At Issue

| The CIA

Other books in the At Issue series:

At Issue

The CIA

Julia Bauder, Book Editor

GREENHAVEN PRESS

An imprint of Thomson Gale, a part of The Thomson Corporation

Detroit • New York • San Francisco • New Haven, Conn. • Waterville, Maine • London

Christine Nasso, *Publisher*
Elizabeth Des Chenes, *Managing Editor*

© 2007 The Gale Group.

Star logo is a trademark and Gale and Greenhaven Press are registered trademarks used herein under license.

For more information, contact:
Greenhaven Press
27500 Drake Rd.
Farmington Hills, MI 48331-3535
Or you can visit our Internet site at http://www.gale.com

LIBRARY OF CONGRESS CATALOGING-IN-PUBLICATION DATA

The CIA / Julia Bauder, book editor.
    p. cm. -- (At issue)
Includes bibliographical references and index.
ISBN-13: 978-0-7377-3677-9 (hardcover)
ISBN-13: 978-0-7377-3678-6 (pbk.)
    1. United States. Central Intelligence Agency--Juvenile literature. I. Bauder, Julia
JK468.I6C23 2007
327.1273--dc22
                                                    2007025905

ISBN-10: 0-7377-3677-1 (hardcover)
ISBN-10: 0-7377-3678-X (pbk.)

Printed in the United States of America
10 9 8 7 6 5 4 3 2 1

Contents

Introduction

In the American popular imagination, the Central Intelligence Agency (CIA) is synonymous with spying. In books, movies, and television shows, nearly everything the American government does that involves espionage, covert operations, or any other shady work is carried out by CIA agents.

Yet in reality the CIA is only one small part of the American intelligence community. The size of the CIA's budget and the number of employees who work for it are secret, so no one outside the government knows precisely how large the CIA is. General agreement, however, is that the CIA is dwarfed by the fifteen other U.S. intelligence agencies that together with the CIA make up the U.S. intelligence community:

- The Air Intelligence Agency, Army Intelligence, the Marine Corps Intelligence Agency, and the Office of Naval Intelligence. These four agencies are primarily concerned with gathering the intelligence that the leaders of the four branches of the military need to plan and carry out military operations, such as locating targets and predicting the actions of opposing forces, but information gathered by these agencies may also be shared across the intelligence community.

- The Defense Intelligence Agency, which gathers military-related intelligence for use by both the military and policy makers.

- The National Geospatial-Intelligence Agency, which is part of the Department of Defense. This agency was created in 1996 to centralize the collection of geographic imagery and the creation of maps for use by the military and other intelligence agencies.

- The National Reconnaissance Office, which was created in 1960 to oversee the use of satellites to spy on foreign countries. The office is also part of the Department of Defense.

- The National Security Agency (NSA), which is the largest single U.S. intelligence agency. The NSA focuses on signals intelligence (often referred to as SIGINT)—eavesdropping on communications. It, too, is part of the Department of Defense.

- The Drug Enforcement Administration's (DEA) Office of National Security Intelligence, which handles intelligence gathered in the course of the agency's fight against international drug trafficking. It is part of the Department of Justice.

- The Federal Bureau of Investigation's (FBI) Directorate of Intelligence, which focuses on intelligence about crimes and terrorist threats within the United States. It is also part of the Department of Justice.

- The U.S. Department of Energy's Office of Intelligence, which gathers intelligence related to nuclear energy, nuclear weapons, energy security, and other scientific and technical areas.

- The U.S. Department of Homeland Security, which contains two intelligence agencies: Coast Guard Intelligence and the Office of Intelligence and Analysis, which is responsible for collecting and analyzing information gathered by the other intelligence agencies about terrorist threats within the United States.

- The U.S. Department of State's Bureau of Intelligence and Research, which supplies intelligence analyses to the State Department's diplomats.

- The U.S. Department of the Treasury's Office of Intelligence and Analysis, which attempts to track the funding of terrorist groups, rogue states, and drug traffickers.

The CIA's position within this alphabet soup of agencies has always been precarious. The CIA was created to be the "central" agency, responsible for collecting and analyzing information gathered by all of the other agencies, and its director was intended to be the head of the entire intelligence community. The director of the CIA, however, has never had any effective power over the other agencies. In addition, many of the CIA's responsibilities overlap with those of the other agencies of the intelligence community, often making it unclear who is, or ought to be, ultimately in charge of any particular area of intelligence.

After the September 11, 2001, terrorist attacks, this fragmented intelligence system came under close scrutiny. Blame for the intelligence failures that led to the attacks was spread across multiple agencies, and many of the proposed solutions also involved making wholesale changes in the entire intelligence community. The goal, proponents of these proposed solutions said, was to streamline the intelligence system and promote better cooperation among the various agencies.

Congress passed a version of these proposals, the Intelligence Reform and Terrorism Prevention Act, in 2004. This legislation created a director of national intelligence (DNI), separate from the director of central intelligence (the head of the CIA), to oversee the intelligence community, and gave the DNI real power over the agencies. It also created a new organization, the National Counterterrorism Center, which was intended to bring together all of the intelligence and other government agencies that had a role to play in fighting terrorism.

Although popular opinion was that some changes in the American intelligence system were necessary, these specific changes have been controversial. The idea that centralizing the intelligence community will improve American intelligence is popular, but some dissenters believe that this centralization may make the CIA and the other individual intelligence agencies less effective. Others have argued that the changes made by the Intelligence Reform and Terrorism Prevention Act do not address the real roots of U.S. intelligence failures and have proposed entirely different sets of reforms for the CIA. These topics are among the issues debated by the authors in *At Issue: The Central Intelligence Agency.*

1

The CIA:
An Overview

Office of the Director of National Intelligence

The Office of the Director of National Intelligence is a new federal agency, created in 2005, to oversee the fourteen agencies that make up the United States intelligence community.

The Central Intelligence Agency (CIA) was created in 1947 to serve the president and other government officials by providing them with information and analyses about foreign affairs and national security threats. In order to carry out this mission, the CIA is divided into four directorates that each focuses on one aspect of the intelligence process: the National Clandestine Service, which carries out undercover operations; the Directorate of Intelligence, which analyzes information gathered from a variety of sources; the Directorate of Science and Technology, which researches and implements technology-based methods of gathering intelligence; and the Directorate of Support, which provides services that help the other three directorates to function efficiently.

The Central Intelligence Agency (CIA), established by the National Security Act of 1947, is responsible to the President through the Director of National Intelligence and accountable to the American people through the Intelligence Oversight Committees of the Congress. The Director of CIA (DCIA) also serves as the National HUMINT [human intelligence] Manager.

Excerpt from *An Overview of the United States Intelligence Community*. Washington, DC: Office of the Director of National Intelligence, 2006.

The core mission of the CIA is to support the President, the National Security Council, and all officials who make and execute US national security policy by:

- Providing accurate, comprehensive, and timely foreign intelligence and analysis on national security topics.

- Conducting counterintelligence activities, special activities, and other functions related to foreign intelligence and national security as directed by the President.

To accomplish the mission, CIA works closely with the rest of the Intelligence Community [IC] and other government agencies to ensure that intelligence consumers—whether administration policymakers, diplomats, or military commanders—receive the best intelligence possible.

The Divisions of the CIA

The CIA is organized into four mission components called Directorates, which together carry out "the intelligence process"—the cycle of collecting, analyzing, and disseminating intelligence:

The National Clandestine Service (NCS)

The National Clandestine Service is the clandestine arm of the CIA. Its core mission is to support our country's security and foreign policy interests by conducting clandestine activities to collect information that is not obtainable through other means. The information the NCS collects is reviewed for reliability before its dissemination to policymakers. Although the primary focus of the NCS is the collection and dissemination of foreign intelligence, it also conducts counterintelligence activities abroad and special activities as authorized by the President. The Director of the National Clandestine Service (D/NCS) serves as the national authority for the integration, coordination, de-confliction, and evaluation of clandestine HUMINT operations across the Intelligence Community, under the authorities delegated to the Director of the CIA as the National HUMINT Manager. As part of its Community responsibilities, the NCS develops common standards for all aspects of clandestine human intelligence operations, including human-enabled technical operations, across the IC. The DNCS also oversees the Central Intelligence Agency's clandestine operations.

The Directorate of Intelligence (DI)

The Directorate of Intelligence supports the President, administration policymakers, the Congress, Pentagon planners and war fighters, law enforcement agencies, and negotiators with timely, comprehensive, all-source intelligence analysis about a wide range of national security issues. The DI integrates, analyzes, and evaluates information collected through clandestine and other means, including open sources, to generate value-added insights. The substantive scope of the DI is worldwide and covers functional as well as regional issues; its products range from quick-reaction, informal oral briefings to complex, long-term research studies. The DI works closely with the NCS and other collectors to enhance the quality and timeliness of intelligence support to consumers. This partnership provides a single focal point within CIA for the consumer and also strengthens CIA's analytical efforts in support of policymakers' needs.

The Directorate of Science
and Technology (DS&T)

The Directorate of Science and Technology works closely with the National Clandestine Service an Directorate of Intelligence to access, collect, and exploit critical intelligence by applying innovative scientific, engineering, and technical solutions. DS&T officers are actively engaged in programs to assure clandestine access to intelligence targets worldwide, to obtain intelligence through technical means, to provide technical support to clandestine operations, and to discover new technologies that will enhance our nation's ability to gain insight into the activities of our adversaries. The Director for Science and Technology is the senior scientific and technical adviser to the Director of the Central Intelligence Agency. The DS&T also serves as the Executive Agent for In-Q-Tel, the nonprofit, strategic venture capital firm chartered to connect the technology demands of the CIA and IC partners' intelligence missions with the emerging technology of the entrepreneurial community. The DS&T maintains extensive contacts with the scientific and technical communities nationwide and has the capability to rapidly assemble experts in many fields in order to bring the technological prowess of the US to bear on fast-breaking intelligence and national security issues.

The Directorate of Support (DS)

The Directorate of Support provides integrated, mission-critical support to the National Clandestine Service, the Directorate of Intelligence, the Directorate of Science and Technology, and across the Intelligence Community. The DS's core support disciplines include human resources, financial and logistical operations, medical support, contracts and acquisitions, security, secretarial and administrative support, facilities, and integrated information technology support. The Directorate has a significant number of professional certifications, including doctors, lawyers, accountants, engineers, law enforcement officers, and architects. Its workforce supports the CIA's mission worldwide, providing 24/7 support that is international in focus and clandestine in nature. About half of the DS's workforce is embedded within their various mission partners, with the largest concentration serving in the National Clandestine Service and across the Intelligence Community. The DS maintains a broad range of capabilities in order to support CIA's unique mission.

2

The CIA Tortures Prisoners in the War on Terror

Jane Mayer

Jane Mayer is a staff writer for the New Yorker.

Since September 11, 2001, the U.S. government has created new guidelines that appear to allow Central Intelligence Agency (CIA) agents to torture and even kill prisoners with impunity. Under these guidelines an Iraqi prisoner suffocated to death while being interrogated by a CIA agent, who has not been charged with any crimes in the death.

At the end of a secluded cul-de-sac, in a fast-growing Virginia suburb favored by employees of the Central Intelligence Agency, is a handsome replica of an old-fashioned farmhouse, with a white-railed front porch. The large back yard has a swimming pool, which, on a recent October afternoon, was neatly covered. In the driveway were two cars, a late-model truck, and an all-terrain vehicle. The sole discordant note was struck by a faded American flag on the porch; instead of fluttering in the autumn breeze, it was folded on a heap of old Christmas ornaments.

The house belongs to Mark Swanner, a forty-six-year-old C.I.A. officer who has performed interrogations and polygraph tests for the agency, which has employed him at least since the nineteen-nineties. (He is not a covert operative.) Two years ago, at Abu Ghraib prison, outside Baghdad, an Iraqi prisoner in Swanner's custody, Manadel al-Jamadi, died during an interrogation. His head had been covered with a plastic bag, and he was shackled in a crucifixion-like pose that inhibited his ability to breathe; according to forensic pathologists who have examined the case, he asphyxiated. In a subsequent internal investigation, United States government authorities classified Jamadi's death as a "homicide," meaning that it resulted from unnatural causes. Swanner has not been charged with a crime and continues to work for the agency.

After September 11th, the justice Department fashioned secret legal guidelines that appear to indemnify C.I.A. officials who perform aggressive, even violent interrogations outside the United States. Techniques such as waterboarding—the near-drowning of a suspect—have been implicitly authorized by an Administration [headed by George W. Bush] that feels that such methods may be necessary to win the war on terrorism. (In 2001, Vice-President Dick Cheney, in an interview on "Meet the Press," said that the government might have to go to "the dark side" in handling terrorist suspects, adding, "It's going to be vital for us to use any means at our disposal.") The harsh treatment of Jamadi and other prisoners in C.I.A. custody, however, has inspired an emotional debate in Washington, raising questions about what limits should be placed on agency officials who interrogate foreign terrorist suspects outside U.S. territory. . . .

The C.I.A. has reportedly been implicated in at least four deaths of detainees in Afghanistan and Iraq.

Manadel al-Jamadi was captured by Navy SEALS [sea, air, land team] at 2 a.m. on November 4, 2003, after a violent struggle at his house, outside Baghdad [Iraq], Jamadi savagely fought one of the SEALS before being subdued in his kitchen; during the altercation, his stove fell on them. The C.I.A. had identified him as a "high-value" target, because he had allegedly supplied the explosives used in several atrocities perpetrated by insurgents, including the bombing of the Baghdad headquarters of the International Committee of the Red Cross, in October, 2003. After being removed from his house, Jamadi was manhandled by several of the SEALS, who gave him a black eye and a cut on his face; he was then transferred to C.I.A. custody, for interrogation at Abu Ghraib. According to witnesses, Jamadi was walking and speaking when he arrived at the prison. He was taken to a shower room for interrogation. Some forty-five minutes later, he was dead. . . .

A government official familiar with the case, who declined to be named, indicated that establishing guilt in the case might be complicated, because of Jamadi's rough handling by the SEALS before he entered the custody of the C.I.A. Yet, in the past two years, several of the Navy SEALS who captured Jamadi and delivered him to C.I.A. officials have faced abuse charges in military-justice proceedings, and have been exonerated. Moreover, three medical experts who have examined Jamadi's case told me that the injuries he sustained from the SEALS could not have caused his death.

Secret Prisons and Unaccountable Interrogators

Since September 11, 2001, the C.I.A.'s treatment and interrogation of terrorist suspects has remained almost entirely hidden from public view. Human-rights groups estimate that some ten thousand foreign suspects are being held in U.S. detention facilities in Afghanistan, Iraq, Cuba, and other countries. A small but unknown part of this population is in the custody of the C.I.A., which, as Dana Priest reported recently [2005] in the *Washington Post*, has operated secret prisons in Thailand and in Eastern Europe. It is also unclear how seriously the agency deals with allegations of prisoner abuse. The C.I.A. tends to be careful about following strict legal procedures, including the briefing of the top-ranking members of the congressional intelligence committees on its covert activities. But experts could recall no instance of a C.I.A. officer being tried in a public courtroom for manslaughter or murder. Thomas Powers, the author of two books about the C.I.A., told me, "I've never heard of anyone at the C.I.A. being convicted of a killing." He added that a case such as Jamadi's had awkward political implications. "Is the C.I.A. capable of addressing an illegal killing by its own hands?" he asked. "My guess is not." Whereas the military has subjected itself to a dozen internal investigations in the aftermath of the Abu Ghraib scandal, and has punished more than two hundred soldiers for wrongdoing, the agency has undertaken almost no public self-examination.

The C.I.A. has reportedly been implicated in at least four deaths of detainees in Afghanistan and Iraq including that of Jamadi, and has referred eight potentially criminal cases involving abuse and misconduct to the Justice Department. In March [2005], [Porter] Goss, the C.I.A.'s director, testified before Congress that "we don't do torture," and the agency's press office issued a release stating, "All approved interrogation techniques, both past and present, are lawful and do not constitute torture. . . . C.I.A. policies on interrogation have always followed legal guidance from the Department of Justice. If an individual violates the policy, then he or she will be held accountable."

Even if the [C.I.A.] wanted to discipline or prosecute agents . . . the legal tools to do so may no longer exist.

Yet the government has brought charges against only one person affiliated with the agency: David Passaro, a low-level contract employee, not a full-fledged C.I.A. officer. In 2003, Passaro, while interrogating an Afghan prisoner, allegedly beat him with a flashlight so severely that he eventually died from his injuries. In two other incidents of prisoner abuse, the [New York] Times reported last month, charges probably will not be brought against C.I.A. personnel: the 2003 case of an Iraqi prisoner who was forced head first into a sleeping bag, then beaten; and the 2002 abuse of an Afghan prisoner who froze to death after being stripped and chained to the floor of a concrete cell. (The C.I.A. supervisor involved in the latter case was subsequently promoted.)

Permission to Torture

One reason these C.I.A. officials may not be facing charges is that, in recent years, the Justice Department has established a strikingly narrow definition of torture. In August, 2002, the department's Office of Legal Counsel sent a memo on interrogations to the White House, which argued that a coercive technique was torture only when it induced pain equivalent to what a person experiencing death or organ failure might suffer. By implication, all lesser forms of physical and psychological mistreatment—what critics have called "torture lite"—were legal. The memo also said that torture was illegal only when it could be proved that the interrogator intended to cause the required level of pain. And it provided interrogators with another large exemption: torture might be acceptable if an interrogator was acting in accordance with military "necessity." A source familiar with the memo's origins, who declined to speak on the record, said that it "was written as an immunity, a blank check." In 2004, the "torture memo," as it became known, was leaked. . . . The Administration subsequently revised the guidelines, using language that seemed more restrictive. But a little-noticed footnote protected the coercive methods permitted by the "torture memo," stating that they did not violate the "standards set forth in this memorandum."

The Bush Administration has resisted disclosing the contents of two Justice Department memos that established a detailed interrogation policy for the Pentagon and the C.I.A. A March, 2003, classified memo was "breathtaking," the same source said. The document dismissed virtually all national and international laws regulating the treatment of prisoners, including war-crimes and assault statutes, and it was radical in its view that in wartime the President can fight enemies by whatever means he sees fit. According to the memo, Congress has no constitutional right to interfere with the President in his role as Commander-in-Chief, including making laws that limit the ways in which prisoners may be interrogated. Another classified Justice Department memo, issued in August, 2002, is said to authorize numerous "enhanced" interrogation techniques for the C.I.A. These two memos sanction such extreme measures that, even if the agency wanted to discipline or prosecute agents who stray beyond its own comfort level, the legal tools to do so may no longer exist. . . .

The Roots of U.S. Torture

By the summer of 2003, the insurgency against the U.S. occupation of Iraq had grown into a confounding and lethal insurrection, and the Pentagon and the White House were pressing C.I.A. agents and members of the Special Forces to get the kind of intelligence needed to crush it. On orders from Secretary of Defense Donald Rumsfeld, General Geoffrey Miller, who had overseen coercive interrogations of terrorist suspects at [the U.S. Naval base at] Guantánamo [Bay, Cuba] imposed similar methods at Abu Ghraib [prison in Iraq]. In October of that year, however—a month before Jamadi's death—the Justice Department's Office of Legal Counsel issued an opinion stating that Iraqi insurgents were covered by the Geneva Conventions, which require the humane treatment of prisoners and forbid coercive interrogations. The ruling reversed an earlier interpretation, which had concluded, erroneously, that Iraqi insurgents were not protected by international law.

As a result of these contradictory mandates from Washington, the rules of engagement at Abu Ghraib became muddy, and the tactics grew increasingly ad hoc. Jeffrey H. Smith, a former general counsel of the C.I.A., told me, "Abu Ghraib has its roots at the top. I think this uncertainty about who was and who was not covered by the Geneva Conventions, and all this talk that they're all terrorists, bred the climate in which this kind of abuse takes place.". . .

Jamadi's Arrival

Manadel al-Jamadi arrived at Abu Ghraib naked from the waist down, according to an eyewitness, Jason Kenner, an M.P. [Military Police Officer] with the 372nd Military Police Company. In a statement to C.I.A. investigators, Kenner recalled that Jamadi had been stripped of his pants, underpants, socks, and shoes, arriving in only a purple T-shirt and a purple jacket, and with a green plastic sandbag completely covering his head. Nevertheless, Kenner told C.I.A. investigators, "the prisoner did not appear to be in distress. He was walking fine, and his speech was normal." The plastic "flex cuffs" on Jamadi's wrists were so tight, however, that Kenner had trouble cutting them off when they were replaced with steel handcuffs and Jamadi's hands were secured behind his back.

Staff Sergeant Mark Nagy, a reservist in the 372nd Military Police Company, was also on duty at Abu Ghraib when Jamadi arrived. According to the classified internal documents, he told C.I.A. investigators that Jamadi seemed "lucid," noting that he was "talking during intake." Nagy said that Jamadi was "not combative" when he was placed in a holding cell, and that he "responded to commands." In Nagy's opinion, there was "no need to get physical with him."

Kenner told the investigators that, "minutes" after Jamadi was placed in the holding cell, an "interrogator"—after identified as Swanner—began "yelling at him, trying to find where some weapons were." Kenner said that he could see Jamadi through the open door of the holding cell, "in a seated position like a scared child." The yelling went on, he said, for five or ten minutes. At some point, Kenner said, Swanner and his translator "removed the prisoner's jacket and shirt," leaving him naked. He added that he saw no injuries or bruises. Soon afterward, the M.P.s were told by Swanner and the translator to "take the prisoner to Tier One," the agency's interrogation wing. The M.P.s dressed Jamadi in a standard-issue orange jumpsuit, keeping the sandbag over his head, and walked him to the shower room there for interrogation. Kenner said that Jamadi put up "no resistance."

On the way, Nagy noticed that Jamadi was "groaning and breathing heavily, as if he was out of breath." Walter Diaz, the M.P. who had been on guard duty at the prison, told C.I.A. investigators that Jamadi showed "no distress or complaints on the way to the shower room." But he told me that he, too, noticed that Jamadi was having "breathing problems." An autopsy showed that Jamadi had six fractured ribs; it is unclear when they were broken. The C.I.A. officials in charge of Jamadi did not give him even a cursory medical exam, although the Geneva Conventions require that prisoners receive "medical attention." . . .

Palestinian Hanging

According to Kenner's testimony, when the group reached the shower room Swanner told the M.P.s that "he did not want the prisoner to sit and he wanted him shackled to the wall." (No explanation for this decision is recorded.) There was a barred window on one wall. Kenner and Nagy, using a pair of leg shackles, attached Jamadi's arms, which had been placed behind his back, to the bars on the window.

The Associated Press quoted an expert who described the position in which Jamadi died as a form of torture known as "Palestinian hanging," in which a prisoner whose hands are secured behind his back is suspended by his arms. (The technique has allegedly been used in the Israeli-Palestinian conflict.) The M.P.s' sworn accounts to investigators suggest that, at least at first, Jamadi was able to stand up, without pain: autopsy records show that he was five feet ten, and, as

Diaz explained to me, the window was about five feet off the ground. The accounts concur that, while Jamadi was able to stand without discomfort, he couldn't kneel or sit without hanging painfully from his arms. Once he was secured, the M.P.s left him alone in the room with Swanner and the translator.

Less than an hour later, Diaz said, he was walking past the shower room when Swanner came out and asked for help, reportedly saying, "This guy doesn't want to coöperate.". . . When Diaz entered the shower room, he said, he was surprised to see that Jamadi's knees had buckled, and that he was almost kneeling. Swanner, he said, wanted the soldiers to reposition Jamadi, so that he would have to stand more erectly. Diaz called for additional help from two other soldiers in his company, Sergeant Jeffery Frost and Dennis Stevanus. But after they had succeeded in making Jamadi stand for a moment, as requested, by hitching his handcuffs higher up the window, Jamadi collapsed again. Diaz told me, "At first I was, like, 'This guy's drunk.' He just dropped down to where his hands were, like, coming out of his handcuffs. He looked weird. I was thinking, He's got to be hurting. All of his weight was on his hands and wrists—it looked like he was about to mess up his sockets."

The Death Discovered

Swanner, whom Diaz described as a "kind of shabby-looking, overweight white guy," who was wearing black clothing, was apparently less concerned. "He was saying, 'He's just playing dead,'" Diaz recalled. "He thought he was faking. He wasn't worried at all." While Jamadi hung from his arms, Diaz told me, Swanner "just kept talking and talking at him. But there was no answer."

Frost told C.I.A. investigators that the interrogator had said that Jamadi was just "playing possum." But, as Frost lifted Jamadi upright by his jumpsuit, noticing that it was digging into his crotch, he thought, This prisoner is pretty good at playing possum. When Jamadi's body went slack again, Frost recalled commenting that he "had never seen anyone's arms positioned like that, and he was surprised they didn't just pop out of their sockets."

Diaz, sensing that something was wrong, lifted Jamadi's hood. His face was badly bruised. Diaz placed a finger in front of Jamadi's open eyes, which didn't move or blink, and deduced that he was dead. When the men lowered Jamadi to the floor, Frost told investigators, "blood came gushing out of his nose and mouth, as if a faucet had been turned on."

Attempted Cover-Up?

Swanner, who had seemed so unperturbed, suddenly appeared "surprised" and "dumbfounded," according to Frost. He began talking about how Jamadi had fought and resisted the entire way to the prison. He also made calls on his cell phone. Within minutes, Diaz said, four or five additional O.G.A. ["other government agencies," probably by the C.I.A.] officers, also dressed in black, arrived on the scene. . . .

C.I.A. personnel ordered that Jamadi's body be kept in the shower room until the next morning. The corpse was packed in ice and bound with tape, apparently in an attempt to slow its decomposition and, [Dr. Steven] Miles [a medical ethicist studying medical practices during the war on terrorism] believes, to try to alter the perceived time of death. The ice was already melting when Specialist Sabrina Harman posed for pictures while stooping over Jamadi's body, smiling and giving the thumbs-up sign. The next day, a medic inserted an I.V. in Jamadi's arm, put the body on a stretcher, and took it out of the prison as if Jamadi were merely ill, so as to "not upset the other detainees." Other interrogators, Miles said, "were told that Jamadi had died of a heart attack." (There is no medical evidence that Jamadi experienced heart failure.) A military-intelligence officer later recounted that a local taxi-driver was paid to take away Jamadi's body.

Before leaving, Frost told investigators, Swanner confided that he "did not get any information out of the prisoner." C.I.A. officials took with them the bloodied hood that had covered Jamadi's head; it was later thrown away. "They destroyed evidence, and failed to preserve the scene of the crime," [Frank] Spinner, the lawyer for one of the Navy SEALS, said.

The next day, Swanner gave a statement to Army investigators, stressing that he hadn't laid a hand on Jamadi, and hadn't done anything wrong. "Clint C.," the translator, also said that Swanner hadn't beaten Jamadi. "I don't think anybody intended the guy to die," a former investigator on the case, who asked not to be identified, told me. But he believes that the decision to shackle Jamadi to the window reflected an intent to cause suffering. (Under American and international law, intent is central to assessing criminality in war-crimes and torture cases.) The C.I.A., he said, "put him in that position to get him to talk. They took it that pain equals coöperation."

The autopsy, performed by military pathologists five days later, classified Jamadi's death as a homicide, saying that the cause of death was "compromised respiration" and "blunt force injuries" to Jamadi's head and torso. But it appears that the pathologists who performed the autopsy were unaware that Jamadi had been shackled to a high window. When a description of Jamadi's position was shared with two of the country's most prominent medical examiners—both of whom volunteered to review the autopsy report free, at the request of a lawyer representing one of the SEALS—their conclusion was different. Miles, independently, concurred.

Dr. Michael Baden, who is the chief forensic pathologist for the New York State Police, told me. "What struck me was that Jamadi was alive and well when he walked into the prison. . . ." Jamadi's bruises, he said, were no doubt painful, but they were not life-threatening. Baden went on, "He also had injuries to his ribs. You don't die from broken ribs. But if he had been hung up in this way and had broken ribs, that's different." In his judgment, "asphyxia is what he died from—as in a crucifixion. . . . If his hands were pulled up five feet— that's to his neck. That's pretty tough. That would put a lot of tension on his rib muscles, which are needed for breathing. It's not only painful—it can hinder the diaphragm from going up and down, and the rib cage from expanding. The muscles tire, and the breathing function is impaired, so there's less oxygen entering the bloodstream." A person in such a state would first lose consciousness, he said, and eventually would die. The hood, he suggested, would likely have compounded the problem, because the interrogator "can't see his face if he's turning blue. We see a lot about a patient's condition by look- ing at his face. By putting that goddam hood on, they can't see if he's conscious." It also "doesn't permit them to know when he died." The bottom line, Baden said, is that Jamadi "didn't die as a result of any injury he got before getting to the prison."

Dr. Cyril Wecht, a medical doctor and a lawyer who is the coroner of Allegheny County, Pennsylvania, and a former president of the American Academy of Forensic Sciences, in- dependently reached the same conclusion. The interpretation put forward by the military pathologists, he said, "didn't fit with their own report. They said he died of blunt-force trauma, yet there was no significant evidence of trauma to the head." Instead, Wecht believes that Jamadi "died of compro- mised respiration," and that "the position the body was in would have been the cause of death." He added, "Mind you, I'm not a critic of the Iraq war. But I don't think we should reduce ourselves to the insurgents' barbaric levels."

Walter Diaz told me, "Someone should be charged. If Ja- madi was already handcuffed, there was no reason to treat the guy the way they did—the way they hung him." Diaz said he didn't know if Swanner had intended to torture Jamadi, or whether the death was accidental. But he was troubled by the government's inaction, and by what he saw as the agency's attempt at a coverup. "They tried to blame the SEALS. The C.I.A. had a big role in this. But you know the C.I.A.—who's going to go against them?"

Prosecution Is Unlikely

According to Jeffrey Smith, the former general counsel of the C.I.A., now a private-practice lawyer who handles national-security cases, a decision to prosecute Swanner "would probably go all the way up to the Attorney General." Critics of the Administration, such as John Sifton, a lawyer for Human Rights Watch, question whether Alberto Gonzales, who became Attorney General last year [2004], has too many conflicts of interest to weigh the case against Swanner fairly. Sifton said, "It's hard to imagine the current leadership pursuing these guys, because the head of the Justice Department, Alberto Gonzales, is centrally implicated in crafting the policies that led to the abuse.". . .

Even more troubling is the possibility that, under the Bush Administration's secret interrogation guidelines, the killing of Jamadi might not have broken any laws. Jeffrey Smith says it's possible that the Office of Legal Counsel's memos may have opened too many loopholes for interrogators like Swanner, "making prosecution somehow too hard to do." Smith added, "But, even under the expanded definition of torture, I don't see how someone beaten with his hands bound, who then died while hanging—how that could be legal. I'd be embarrassed if anyone argued that it was."

3

The CIA Kidnaps Suspects and Sends Them to Third Countries to Be Tortured

Stephen Grey

Stephen Grey is a Great Britain-based freelance journalist. He is also the author of Ghost Plane: The True Story of the CIA Torture Program.

The Central Intelligence Agency (CIA) has been seizing people around the world and sending them to third countries, where they are often tortured. Both the arrests themselves and the transfers to countries where torture is known to occur are illegal under international law.

8 *October 2002.* Over the Atlantic, at 30,000 feet, on board a Gulfstream jet, Maher Arar looked out through the portholes of the private plane at the clouds beneath and the red glow of dawn. Stretching out on the wide, upholstered leather seat, he glanced across at the large video screen on which was displayed the path of the plane from its departure point near New York, onwards to Washington, DC and then to its final refuelling point at Portland, Maine, before heading across the ocean. A telecommunications engineer in Ottawa, Canada, Maher was used to air travel—but not to such luxury.

His companions—specialists attached to the CIA—were preparing to switch on another in-flight film, an action movie.

Stephen Grey, "America's Gulag," *New Statesman*, May 17, 2004. Copyright © 2004 New Statesman, Ltd. Reproduced by permission.

Maher could think only of what fate lay ahead of him when he reached the country to where the United States was now sending him for interrogation and from where his family had once fled—Syria.

He recalls: "I knew that Syria was a country that tortured its prisoners. I was silent and submissive; just asking myself over and over again: 'How did I end up in this situation? What is going to happen to me now?'"

The Case of Maher Arar

Maher had been arrested after arriving at New York's JFK Airport at 2 pm on 26 September to change planes. He'd been returning home from a holiday in Tunisia. He was accused of membership of [terrorist] Osama Bin Laden's al-Qaeda organisation and of knowing two other Syrian-Canadians who were said to be terrorists. Maher was baffled; he hardly knew the pair. They both seemed ordinary Muslims like him—hardly extremists.

Though Maher was a Canadian citizen, after interrogation in New York he was told he would be deported to Syria, not his adopted country. It petrified him.

Hundreds [of prisoners] have been transferred [by the CIA] from one Middle Eastern or Asian country to another—countries where prisoners can be more easily interrogated.

One of the CIA agents, who called himself Mr. Khoury, had explained that he, too, was originally from Syria. Unlike Maher, Khoury was wearing a grey lounge suit. Maher was still wearing an orange boiler suit and was shackled with steel handcuffs and chains. During the flight, Khoury lent him a turquoise polo shirt, made in Canada. Maher would be wearing that shirt and nothing else for the next three months. He would be wearing it as his arms, his palms and the soles of his feet were beaten with electric cables.

After the plane landed in Jordan, he was taken by van to a Damascus jail. He was not alone: from the cells around him, he heard the screams of those under torture. One prisoner was from Spain, another from Germany. All had been flown in to help America's war on terrorism.

There was no daylight coming into his cell, just a dim glow through a hole in the reinforced concrete of his ceiling. Maher wanted to pray towards Mecca, but no guard would tell him which direction that was. And anyway, he could bend only one way—forward, towards the metal door. He couldn't keep track of the days, but knew that about once a week, he would be brought out to wash himself.

Secret Flights

Maher was inside a secret system. His flight was on a jet operated for the CIA by the US's Special Collection Service. It runs a fleet of luxury planes, as well as regular military transports, that has moved thousands of prisoners around the world since 11 September 2001—much as the CIA-run secret fleet, Air America, did in the 1960s and 1970s. Some of the prisoners have gone to Guantanamo, the US interrogation centre at its naval base in Cuba. Hundreds more have been transferred from one Middle Eastern or Asian country to another—countries where the prisoners can be more easily interrogated.

For transfers of low-level prisoners from war zones such as Afghanistan and Pakistan, military cargo planes have been used. But the CIA has tended to favour the Gulfstream and other executive jets for the higher-value prisoners and their transfer to sensitive locations. The operations of this airline—and the prisoners that it transports around the world—have been protected in a shroud of total secrecy.

The airline's operations are embarrassing because they highlight intense cooperation with regimes of countries such as Egypt, Syria and Pakistan, which are criticised for their human rights record. The movements of these planes expose a vast archipelago of prison camps and centres where America can carry out torture by proxy. The operations are illegal, in that they violate the anti-torture convention promoted by George W. Bush, which prohibits the transfer of suspects abroad for torture.

Secret Prisons

When Alexander Solzhenitsyn wrote *The Gulag Archipelago*, he described a physical chain of island prisons clustered in Soviet Russia's northern seas and in Siberia. But the description was also metaphorical: the archipelago was a cluster of prisons around which swirled the sea of normal society.

Just like Solzhenitsyn's system, the American archipelago operates as a secret network that remains largely unseen by the world. Although a few of the prisons have become well-known—Guantanamo, in Cuba; the CIA interrogation centre at the US air-base in Bagram [Afghanistan], just north of Kabul; the airbase on British Diego Garcia—there are others, hidden from view: the floating interrogation centre located on board a US naval vessel in the Indian Ocean; an unknown jail referred to only as Hotel California by the CIA. Of those operated by America's allies, the worst prisons include the Scorpion jail and the Lazoghly Square secret police headquarters in Cairo, [Egypt,] and the Far Falastin interrogation centre in Damascus, Syria.

The transfer to these prisons, unregulated by any law, has become known as "rendition", a term used as an alternative to lawful "extradition". Rendition was invented by Sandy Berger, Bill Clinton's national security adviser, who described it as a "new art form". After 9/11, a trickle of renditions became a flow, and became the foundation of a whole system to tackle world terrorism. J. Cofer Black, former head of the CIA's counter-terrorism centre, testified in late 2002 that there were at least 3,000 terrorist prisoners being held worldwide.

Intelligence documents show the scale may be even greater. In the two years following 9/11, the Sudanese intelligence service alone claimed to have sent more than 200 captured prisoners into US custody. Of the terrorist suspects seized by America in the same period, only US citizens such as John Walker Lindh, the Californian found fighting with the Taliban, or those arrested within the US, such as Zacarias Moussaoui, accused of being a would-be hijacker in the 9/11 attack, would make it to court.

Battlefield Arrests

Tora Bora, Afghanistan, early December 2001. Up in the foothills of the Spin Ghar mountains on the border between Afghanistan and Pakistan, a British special forces soldier reaches into his pocket to find his tangle of plastic handcuffs. Grabbing his prisoner's arms, he locks them tight around the wrists.

Daylight reveals the detritus of a night fight—four hours of battle that have been the SAS's [Special Air Service, a British special forces unit] biggest engagement since Yemen in 1972. On the churned-up slopes of rough grass and patches of snow, blankets, personal belongings, empty shell casings and the bodies of 38 Islamic warriors lie abandoned.

Operating outside the law, the CIA has established snatch squads around the world.

Another 22 fighters, the survivors, are kneeling on the ground. The fighters, from across Arabia, from Pakistan and even from Chechnya, are dressed in brown and grey shalwar kameez and thin sandals. Their hands are tied behind their backs, held taut with plasticuffs. Their heads are covered with canvas bags.

These arrests provided the entry point into the American archipelago. Though Britain and other allies would later criticise America's tactics and its treatment of terror prisoners (the British high court would call it "monstrous"), this operation proved how UK soldiers were involved with US activities from the beginning. New sources reveal the extent of the involvement—from Britain's participation in Task Force 11, a special forces group operating from a base code-named K2 in Uzbekistan, to a series of SAS battles in Afghanistan that resulted in the capture of large numbers of prisoners.

As a "combat zone", Afghanistan provided some legal cover for those arrests. But Britain and America also seized many others across the border in Pakistan.

Operating outside the law, the CIA has established snatch squads around the world. They have allowed the arrests of suspects, including Britons, which would be illegal if they took place on home soil. For instance, Wahab al-Rawi, a Briton, was questioned, but never arrested or held by MI5 [Britain's national security agency] in the UK. He came to be arrested only following a tip-off from MI5 to the CIA when he visited the Gambia, in West Africa, where legal controls were more lax.

The Case of Wahab al-Rawi

Wahab al-Rawi is Iraqi-born, but a British citizen. He is enormous, and cannot walk too far without running out of breath. "I was fat before the Americans arrested me," he quips.

Wahab sits in a jail cell in the Gambian capital, Banjul, at the headquarters of the country's secret police. His questioner is an American "from the embassy", who, it is pretty clear, works for the CIA. Wahab has been answering questions about his supposed membership of al-Qaeda. He later describes his interrogator thus: "He called himself Mr. Lee and was even bigger than me. He was so enormous he had these rolls of fat like breasts."

Wahab, a 38-year-old from Acton, west London, has been in jail for the past four days. He was arrested at the airport when he went to greet his brother, Bisher, coming in on a flight from London. A businessman whose family fled persecution from Saddam Hussein in Iraq, he had invested (£) 300,000 [nearly $600,000] after mortgaging his house to back his latest business venture: a mobile factory to process Gambian peanuts. Bisher, who is handy with anything technical, had come out to help fix up the equipment.

Across the world, the involvement of the CIA in the arrest of suspects, typically bypassing local laws, has become routine.

Like Canada's Maher Arar, Wahab and Bisher got into trouble after surveillance information was passed to the US by their domestic intelligence agency—in their case, MI5. Both Wahab and Bisher are friends with a Jordanian Islamic preacher in London called Abu Qatada who is accused of having links to terrorists. Abu Qatada is eventually locked up by the British, but there is insufficient (or no) evidence to arrest or hold Wahab or Bisher. Instead, their details are passed on to the US as part of an "intelligence exchange" in the post-11 September world.

"When I asked Lee whether I could see the British consul to protest at my arrest, he laughed," recalls Wahab. "Why do you think you're here?' he asked me. 'It's your government that tipped us off in the first place.'"

The CIA official was thereby breaching the Vienna Convention, which requires foreign detainees to get access to their nation's consulate.

Illegal Arrests

Across the world, the involvement of the CIA in the arrest of suspects, typically bypassing local laws, has become routine.

After Bosnia's civil war, which killed more than 200,000 people, the US and Europe worked hard to instil the idea that disputes should be solved through legal channels. But the CIA disregarded the new Bosnian supreme court and took four suspects away for questioning. In Malawi, which receives British and US development aid to foster the growth of a legal system, a local court was ignored when the CIA snatched four al-Qaeda suspects last year. The men were released after interrogation.

Rendition arrests probably began in earnest in Tirana, Albania, in July 1998 when a team of CIA operatives ran an operation with Albania's secret police. They tracked down and tailed a group of five Egyptian Islamist militants, foiling their plan to destroy the US embassy with a truck bomb. They were captured together and taken to police headquarters where, as the CIA waited outside, they were physically tortured. They were then bundled into an unmarked US Gulfstream jet waiting at the airport and flown to Cairo.

After being handed over to the Egyptian government, Ahmed Osman Saleh was suspended from the ceiling and given electric shocks; he was later hanged after a trial in absentia. Mohamed Hassan Tita was hung by his wrists and given electric shocks to his feet and back. Shawki Attiya was given electric shocks to his genitals, suspended by his limbs and made to stand for hours in filthy water up to his knees. Ahmad Ibrahim al-Naggar was kept in a room with water up to his knees for 35 days; had electric shocks to his nipples and penis; and was hanged without trial in February 2000.

Torture in Syria

15 December 2002, downtown Damascus, Syria. In a bustling street, taxis are honking their horns. Pedestrians hurry by. They hurry because no one on this road likes to linger too long. The office building beside the road—with its tinted windows—has a certain reputation. It is the headquarters of the Mukhabarat, foreign intelligence.

Elsewhere in the city, the atmosphere is relaxed today. The president, the young London-educated former eye doctor Bashar al-Assad, is back in London with his British wife, Asma (or "Emma", as she used to call herself), on a state visit to see Tony Blair and the Queen.

The previous night, al-Assad has been at the Lord Mayor's Banquet, where business leaders and politicians toasted Syria's commitment to peace and reform. Blair welcomes al-Assad with lunch at Downing Street and the Syrian president enthuses about "the warm personal relations I enjoy with Mr Blair".

Maher Arar has no access to radio or television to hear news of the rapprochement between the two countries. He is still in his cell, barely wider than his torso and about two inches longer than his height.

As Blair sits down to chat to al-Assad about progress on the war on the terror and the need to support the US/UK plan to invade Iraq, Arar is reaching the end of his tether. For days he has endured beatings, constant questioning and demands that he confess. He is, in fact, ready to confess to anything. He signs a false statement saying that he went for training in Afghanistan. But what he cannot do—because he knows nothing—is provide useful information that the Syrians can pass back to US intelligence.

In the depths of Far'Falastin jail, one floor below the Falastin road, Arar has no contact with other prisoners. All he can hear, during the ten months of his imprisonment, is the sound of them screaming.

In the beginning, the jailers take him upstairs regularly to be questioned and beaten. Before sessions he is placed in a waiting room where he gets to hear the torture of other prisoners. They call out: "Allah-u-allah"—"God, oh God," they cry. Once he hears the sound of someone's head being slammed repeatedly against the metal interrogation table. . . .

The former CIA agent Bob Baer, who worked covertly for the US across the Middle East until the mid-1990s, describes how each Middle Eastern country has a purpose in the archipelago. He says: "If you want a serious interrogation, you send a prisoner to Jordan. If you want them to be tortured, you send them to Syria. If you want someone to disappear—never to see them again—you send them to Egypt."

Torture in Egypt

Cairo, 2003. Each night before sunset, a flotilla of feluccas is untied from jetties in the city centre and sails up against the current on a cool Nile breeze. The boats, filled with tourists, move silently in the calm water. As it grows dark, the tourists may notice a handful of floodlit watchtowers and the silhouettes of guards standing on their turrets, shouldering rifles. Just yards from where they are enjoying the stunning sunset, perhaps discussing their plans for a tour nearby at the Great Pyramids of Giza, is the entrance to what for many is a version of hell.

Behind the walls and watchtowers that announce Torah prison is an inner complex, a 320-cell annex shaped like the letter "H", known as el-Aqrab, or the Scorpion. Some of America's most secret prisoners are held in solitary confinement here. And here, too—for years—some of the most infamous names in Islamist extremism have been held, from the Cairo-born doctor Ayman al-Zawahiri, who became Osama Bin Laden's right-hand man, to Sayyid Qutb, the intellectual extremist who defined the philosophy that has inspired two generations of Islamist terrorists. Many argue that Torah's harsh conditions have helped to breed this extremism.

But the Scorpion annex is something else again. No outsider knows who is being held within its walls. Since its construction was completed in 1993, no visitor—no family member, no lawyer—has been allowed inside. The Scorpion is where some of the secret prisoners of the war on terror are being held and interrogated.

Former prisoners describe "welcome parties", where soldiers line up to "welcome" new detainees and prisoners with batons, electric shocks and beatings. There are also "search parties", accompanied by humiliating practices such as intimate searches, shaving of hair and beatings. And there are also "farewell parties", when the detainee is beaten by jailers before leaving prison.

There are whispers of another secret prison, newly built, which is also being used for holding al-Qaeda suspects: in Upper Nile, near Aswan.

Egyptian officials speak proudly of what they are doing to help the war on terror. It is the latest phase in a long line of covert US co-operation with the Egyptian government stretching back many years. Egypt still receives about $2 [billion] a year in aid from America, of which $1.3 [billion] is military aid.

Nowadays, the co-operation is geared towards helping Egypt ward off Islamist extremism, and also to escape criticism for its many repressive measures.

Normally, all prisoners of Britain, the US and its allies would have the protection of the law of habeas corpus [which guarantees prisoners the right to have a court decide if their imprisonment is legal]. But US federal judges have argued that enemy aliens do not have these rights and that it is not for the courts to interfere with the military in prosecuting a war by second-guessing whom it chooses to detain and interrogate.

After 9/11 Congress authorised the American president to "use all necessary and appropriate force against those nations, organisations or persons (whom) he determines planned, authorised, committed or aided" those attacks. It further recognised presidential authority to decide on any other actions "to respond to, deter or prevent acts of international terrorism".

Assassination

Counter-terrorism Center, CIA headquarters, Langley, Virginia. 6 November 2002. If the colour picture were not so fuzzy, it would be damned impressive. An eye in the sky at 10,000 feet shows live pictures of a convoy of cars moving down a desert highway 12,000 miles away. The picture is being captured by an unmanned Predator spy plane and conveyed by satellite from the Hadramaut region of Yemen.

Though it is 4 am at the Counter-terrorism Centre, the little operations control booth is crowded, as it always is these days. The technology all around is top-of-the-range: the product of billions of dollars of spending.

At the back of the room stand the CIA's lawyers—always present when life-or-death decisions are to be made. But they have already signed up to what will happen next.

At the centre of the screen are some black cross-hairs. They are already locked on to the car in front. It only remains for Cofer Black, the long-time head of the Counter-terrorism Centre, to give the order. A key turns, a button is pressed and the aptly named "hellfire" missile streaks home. An explosion fills the screen—the camera unshaken on the Predator plane from whose wing the missile has been launched.

The target that night is a wanted terrorist named Abu Ali, aka Qaed Salim Sinan al-Harethi. A few hours later, when his death is confirmed, the agents celebrate their success. However, bystanders are also killed, including a US citizen named Kamal Derwish, from Buffalo, New York State.

Assassination of America's enemies seemed a clever tactic after 9/11. The CIA's political masters ordered it to kill terrorist leaders when it was possible to do so with minimum "collateral damage". It was a return to the bad old days of the Phoenix programme (the documented assassination of thousands by the CIA in Vietnam) and Nicaragua (laying mines in harbours in the 1980s and training "contras").

But it often went wrong.

Throughout the new archipelago, the penalty for involvement in Islamist extremism is frequently death or a life sentence. Trials are usually conducted by a military tribunal, and appeals for clemency to be considered only by the US president.

Resistance to CIA Abuses

In Uzbekistan, a maverick British ambassador, Craig Murray, was put on sick leave after he publicly exposed human rights abuses, including execution of Islamist dissidents by boiling alive. Uzbekistan is one of Britain's and America's closest allies in central Asia because it has provided bases that have enabled operations into Afghanistan. The US is settling in for a long-term presence in return for tolerating human-rights abuses.

In the post-9/11 debate on tactics and policy there has been very little effort to address the roots of terrorism. Rather like the cowboy song—"Don't try to understand 'em/Just rope, throw and brand 'em"—Bush's response to the crisis has been too focused on military retaliation.

The military has defended the use of terror tactics. A former US army colonel, Alex Sands, declared: "The whole point of using special operations is to fight terror with terror. Our guys are trained to do the things that traditionally the other guys have done: kidnap, hijack, infiltrate."

Yet as the world gains glimpses of George W. Bush's archipelago, revulsion at the Americans' modus operandi—and support for the suspects they deliver into the torturers' hands—will grow. Rope, throw and brand 'em may no longer prove a suitable containment policy.

4

The CIA's Treatment of Terrorism Suspects in the War on Terror Is Justified

Condoleezza Rice

Condoleezza Rice is the United States secretary of state.

The U.S. program of capturing suspected terrorists overseas and transporting them to other countries is a legal way of dealing with these suspects. These suspects are taken to other countries in order to put them on trial or to question them, not to torture them. The United States does not torture these detainees, and it does not transport them to countries where it believes that they will be tortured.

The United States and many other countries are waging a war against terrorism. For our country this war often takes the form of conventional military operations in places like Afghanistan and Iraq. Sometimes this is a political struggle, a war of ideas. It is a struggle waged also by our law enforcement agencies. Often we engage the enemy through the cooperation of our intelligence services with their foreign counterparts.

We must track down terrorists who seek refuge in areas where governments cannot take effective action, including where the terrorists cannot in practice be reached by the ordinary processes of law. In such places terrorists have planned the killings of thousands of innocents—in New York City or

Condoleezza Rice, "Remarks Upon Her Departure for Europe," U.S. Department of State, December 5, 2005.

Nairobi [Kenya], in Bali [Indonesia], or London [England], in Madrid [Spain], or Beslan [Russia], in Casablanca [Morocco], or Istanbul [Turkey]. Just two weeks ago I also visited a hotel ballroom in Amman [Jordan], viewing the silent, shattered aftermath of one of those attacks.

The United States, and those countries that share the commitment to defend their citizens, will use every lawful weapon to defeat these terrorists. Protecting citizens is the first and oldest duty of any government. Sometimes these efforts are misunderstood. I want to help all of you understand the hard choices involved, and some of the responsibilities that go with them.

What to Do with Captured Terrorists?

One of the difficult issues in this new kind of conflict is what to do with captured individuals who we know or believe to be terrorists. The individuals come from many countries and are often captured far from their original homes. Among them are those who are effectively stateless, owing allegiance only to the extremist cause of transnational terrorism. Many are extremely dangerous. And some have information that may save lives, perhaps even thousands of lives.

The captured terrorists of the 21st century do not fit easily into traditional systems of criminal or military justice which were designed for different needs. We have to adapt. Other governments are now also facing this challenge.

We consider the captured members of al-Qaida and its affiliates to be unlawful combatants who may be held, in accordance with the law of war, to keep them from killing innocents. We must treat them in accordance with our laws, which reflect the values of the American people. We must question them to gather potentially significant, life-saving, intelligence. We must bring terrorists to justice wherever possible.

For decades, the United States and other countries have used "renditions" to transport terrorist suspects from the country where they were captured to their home country or to other countries where they can be questioned, held, or brought to justice.

In some situations a terrorist suspect can be extradited according to traditional judicial procedures. But there have long been many other cases where, for some reason, the local government cannot detain or prosecute a suspect, and traditional extradition is not a good option. In those cases the local government can make the sovereign choice to cooperate in a rendition. Such renditions are permissible under international law and are consistent with the responsibilities of those governments to protect their citizens.

The United States does not transport, and has not transported, detainees from one country to another for the purpose of interrogation using torture.

Rendition is a vital tool in combating transnational terrorism. Its use is not unique to the United States, or to the current administration [of George W. Bush]. Last year [2004], then Director of Central Intelligence George Tenet recalled that our earlier counterterrorism successes included "the rendition of many dozens of terrorists prior to September 11, 2001."

- Ramzi Youssef masterminded the 1993 bombing of the World Trade Center and plotted to blow up airlines over the Pacific Ocean, killing a Japanese airline passenger in a test of one of his bombs. Once tracked down, a rendition brought him to the United States, where he now serves a life sentence.

- One of history's most infamous terrorists, best known as "Carlos the Jackal," had participated in murders in Europe and the Middle East. He was finally captured in Sudan in 1994. A rendition by the French government brought him to justice in France, where he is now imprisoned. Indeed, the European Commission of Human Rights rejected Carlos' claim that his rendition from Sudan was unlawful.

Renditions take terrorists out of action, and save lives.

Renditions Do Not Lead to Torture

In conducting such renditions, it is the policy of the United States, and I presume of any other democracies who use this procedure, to comply with its laws and comply with its treaty obligations, including those under the Convention Against Torture. Torture is a term that is defined law. We rely on our law to govern our operations. The United States does not permit, tolerate, or condone torture under any circumstances. Moreover, in accordance with the policy of this administration:

- The United States has respected—and will continue to respect—the sovereignty of other countries.

- The United States does not transport, and has not transported, detainees from one country to another for the purpose of interrogation using torture.

- The United States does not use the airspace or the airports of any country for the purpose of transporting a detainee to a country where he or she will be tortured.

- The United States has not transported anyone, and will not transport anyone, to a country when we believe he will be tortured. Where appropriate, the United States seeks assurances that transferred persons will not be tortured.

International law allows a state to detain enemy combatants for the duration of hostilities. Detainees may only be held for an extended period if the intelligence or other evidence against them has been carefully evaluated and supports a determination that detention is lawful. The U.S. does not seek to hold anyone for a period beyond what is necessary to evaluate the intelligence or other evidence against them, prevent further acts of terrorism, or hold them for legal proceedings.

The United States Does Not Torture Prisoners

With respect to detainees, the United States Government complies with its Constitution, its laws, and its treaty obligations. Acts of physical or mental torture are expressly prohibited. The United States Government does not authorize or condone torture of detainees. Torture, and conspiracy to commit torture, are crimes under U.S. law, wherever they may occur in the world.

Violations of these and other detention standards have been investigated and punished. There have been cases of unlawful treatment of detainees, such as the abuse of a detainee by an intelligence agency contractor in Afghanistan or the horrible mistreatment of some prisoners at Abu Ghraib [Iraq] that sickened us all and which arose under the different legal framework that applies to armed conflict in Iraq. In such cases the United States has vigorously investigated, and where appropriate, prosecuted and punished those responsible. Some individuals have already been sentenced to lengthy terms in prison; others have been demoted or reprimanded.

As CIA [Central Intelligence Agency] Director [Porter] Goss recently stated, our intelligence agencies have handled the gathering of intelligence from a very small number of extremely dangerous detainees, including the individuals who planned the 9/11 attacks in the United States, the attack on the U.S.S. *Cole,* and many other murders and attempted murders. It is the policy of the United States that this questioning is to be conducted within U.S. law and treaty obligations, without using torture. It is also U.S. policy that authorized interrogation will be consistent with U.S. obligations under the Convention Against Torture, which prohibit cruel, inhuman, or degrading treatment. The intelligence so gathered has stopped terrorist attacks and saved innocent lives—in Europe as well as in the United States and other countries. The United States has fully respected the sovereignty of other countries that cooperate in these matters.

Debating How to Fight Terrorism

Because this war on terrorism challenges traditional norms and precedents of previous conflicts, our citizens have been discussing and debating the proper legal standards that should apply. President Bush is working with the U.S. Congress to come up with good solutions. I want to emphasize a few key points.

- The United States is a country of laws. My colleagues and I have sworn to support and defend the Constitution of the United States. We believe in the rule of law.

- The United States Government must protect its citizens. We and our friends around the world have the responsibility to work together in finding practical ways to defend ourselves against ruthless enemies. And these terrorists are some of the most ruthless enemies we face.

- We cannot discuss information that would compromise the success of intelligence, law enforcement, and military operations. We expect that other nations share this view.

Some governments choose to cooperate with the United States in intelligence, law enforcement, or military matters. That cooperation is a two-way street. We share intelligence that has helped protect European countries from attack, helping save European lives.

It is up to those governments and their citizens to decide if they wish to work with us to prevent terrorist attacks against their own country or other countries, and decide how much sensitive information they can make public. They have a sovereign right to make that choice.

Debate in and among democracies is natural and healthy. I hope that that debate also includes a healthy regard for the responsibilities of governments to protect their citizens.

Four years after September 11 [2001], most of our populations are asking us if we are doing all that we can to protect them. I know what it is like to face an inquiry into whether everything was done that could have been done. So now, before the next attack, we should all consider the hard choices that democratic governments must face. And we can all best meet this danger if we work together.

5

The CIA Politicized Evidence About Weapons of Mass Destruction in Iraq

James Risen

James Risen is a reporter for the New York Times. *He is also the author of several books, including* State of War: The Secret History of the CIA and the Bush Administration, *from which the following selection is excerpted.*

Before the 2003 invasion of Iraq, the Central Intelligence Agency (CIA) exaggerated the quality of the evidence that it had about Iraq's weapons of mass destruction (WMD) programs. The CIA did this because it felt pressured to support President George W. Bush's policies in the War on Terror, and it believed that expressing doubts about the extent of Iraq's WMD program would be perceived as an attempt to undermine the president. This perceived pressure led the CIA to rely on a single unverified source— who later turned out to be lying—when it claimed that Iraq had an active biological weapons program.

Ever since the U.S. invasion of Iraq and the subsequent discovery that Iraq did not have weapons of mass destruction, officials in the [George W.] Bush administration and the CIA have insisted that they truly believed before the war that those threatening weapons did exist. President Bush and his top advisors have repeatedly claimed that they did not exaggerate the threat, and top CIA officials have publicly argued

James Risen, *State of War: The Secret History of the CIA and the Bush Administration.* New York: Free Press, 2006. Copyright © 2006 by James Risen. Reprinted by permission of the author.

that their ominous assessments that Iraq had ongoing chemical, biological, and nuclear weapons programs were fully justified by the available intelligence.

But in fact, many CIA officials—from rank-and-file analysts to senior managers—knew before the war that they lacked sufficient evidence to make the case for the existence of Iraq's weapons programs. Those doubts were stifled because of the enormous pressure that officials at the CIA and other agencies felt to support the administration. CIA Director George Tenet and his senior lieutenants became so focused on providing intelligence reports that supported the Bush administration's agenda, and so fearful of creating a rift with the White House, that they created a climate within the CIA in which warnings that the available evidence on Iraqi WMD was weak were either ignored or censored. Tenet and his senior aides may not have meant to foster that sort of work environment—and perhaps did not even realize that they were doing it—but the result was that the CIA caught a fatal case of war fever....

Mismanagement

One former CIA official recalled how Tenet's chaotic management style allowed even inexperienced analysts to get their reports directly to the CIA director without adequate vetting by more experienced professionals. Tenet chaired daily meetings on key issues, including both Iraq and counterterrorism, and those conferences were often crowded with mid-level and junior officials eager to get noticed by the director. By presenting their reports during these large conferences with top CIA management, these junior officers were able to short-circuit the normal analytical process. Intelligence reports that seemed to corroborate the administration's agenda could thus go directly from an ambitious junior analyst to George Tenet, who could then take them straight to the White House and George W. Bush. The CIA's mistaken embrace of intelligence claiming that a shipment of aluminum tubes was proof that Saddam

[Hussein] was reconstituting his nuclear weapons program was a prime example of that management disarray.

An attitude took hold among many senior CIA officials that war [with Iraq] was inevitable—and so the quality of intelligence on weapons of mass destruction didn't really matter.

"I was in a meeting chaired by Tenet where you had kids from WINPAC [the CIA's Weapons Intelligence, Nonproliferation, and Arms Control Center]," recalled a former official. During the meeting, the former official recalled, Deputy CIA Director John McLaughlin observed that he had heard that analysts at the Energy Department were skeptical that the aluminum tubes could be used for a nuclear program. "And this young analyst from WINPAC, who didn't look older than twenty-five, says, no, that's bullshit, there is only one use for them," recalled the former official. "And Tenet says, 'yeah? Great.'

"So you had people sprinkled throughout the organization who felt like they could go right to the top, and no one was there to contradict them."

One key nuclear weapons analyst in WINPAC, who has been identified in the press only as "Joe," was one of the primary advocates within the agency arguing that the aluminum tubes were for use in a nuclear weapons program. The CIA had almost no other physical evidence to show that Iraq was developing nuclear weapons, and so Joe's tube intelligence reports brought him high-level attention. CIA sources say Joe was often able to deal directly with McLaughlin, circumventing the normal chain of command. (The independent WMD commission later concluded that the intelligence community's failure on the Iraqi nuclear issue was perhaps the most damaging of any of its errors during the run-up to the Iraq War.)

As the invasion of Iraq drew closer, an attitude took hold among many senior CIA officials that war was inevitable—and so the quality of the intelligence on weapons of mass destruction didn't really matter. This attitude led CIA management to cut corners and accept shoddy intelligence, other CIA officials believe. "One of the senior guys in the NE Division [the Near East Division of the Directorate of Operations [DO]] told me that it isn't going to matter once we go into Baghdad, we are going to find mountains of this stuff," recalled a former CIA official, who left the agency after the war. . . .

An Unreliable Source

The poisonous climate in the U.S. intelligence community during the prewar period was perfect for hustlers and fabricators eager, top their own reasons, to tell tall tales to the Americans. Many of them were Iraqi exiles who reported that Saddam did have WMD. There were warnings given to top CIA officials that some of the Iraqi exiles and defectors were lying, but these warnings were often ignored. Perhaps the most egregious example came in the case of an Iraqi exile who was given the apt code name of Curveball.

The poisonous climate in the U.S. intelligence community . . . was perfect for hustlers and fabricators eager, for their own reasons, to tell tall tales to the Americans.

The information provided by Curveball was critical to the Bush administration's case that Iraq was developing biological weapons. Curveball said that Saddam Hussein's regime had developed mobile biological laboratories that enabled Iraqi scientists to keep their bioweapons out of sight of UN inspectors. Secretary of State Colin Powell relied on information from Curveball in his presentation to the United Nations [UN] in February 2003.

Later, the independent WMD commission concluded that "the intelligence community fundamentally misjudged the status of Iraq's BW [biowarfare] programs" and that the "central basis" for its misguided assessment "was the reporting of a single human source, Curveball," who proved to be a fabricator. The commission observed that "the Curveball story" is one of "poor asset validation by our human collection agencies; of a tendency of analysts to believe that which fits their theories; of inadequate communication between the intelligence community and the policy makers it serves; and ultimately, of poor leadership and management."

The Curveball story is also one of high-level confrontation, between George Tenet and John McLaughlin on one side, and Tyler Drumheller, a genial and rotund man who was the chief of the European Division in the CIA's Directorate of Operations, on the other. Drumheller tried to prevent Curveball's lies from getting into Colin Powell's UN presentation, and his experience provides a vivid glimpse into the hothouse atmosphere at CIA headquarters in the months before the invasion of Iraq.

Third-Hand Reports

Perhaps the most shocking thing about the American reliance on Curveball was the fact that U.S. intelligence officials never even met him before the war and couldn't talk to him directly. Curveball was an Iraqi exile who served as a source for the German intelligence service, and the Germans refused to provide the United States with direct access to the informant. The Germans claimed that Curveball would refuse to talk to the Americans, and so they would only provide reports based on their own debriefings of the Iraqi.

What was worse for the CIA, the agency wasn't even receiving the reports directly from the Germans. Instead, Berlin provided Curveball debriefing reports to a U.S. military intelligence unit, the Defense HUMINT [human intelligence] Service, which then circulated the reports throughout the U.S. intelligence community. Defense HUMINT distributed the reports without any vetting of Curveball's information. The CIA decided it was willing to accept these thirdhand reports.

With no ability to question Curveball and almost no way to corroborate what he was saying, the U.S. intelligence community still fully embraced Curveball's assertions. The October 2002 National Intelligence Estimate [NIE] on Iraq's weapons of mass destruction concluded that Iraq has "transportable facilities for producing bacterial and toxin BW agents." The NIE said it had multiple sources for that assertion, but in fact it was based almost entirely on Curveball.

But even as Curveball's reports were being given the stamp of approval in the NIE, Tyler Drumheller was beginning to hear warnings about the source—from the Germans themselves. As chief of the DO's European Division, Drumheller was in charge of the agency's liaison relationships with Western European intelligence services, and so in the fall of 2002, he had lunch with the Washington station chief of the German intelligence service. With war looming, Drumheller asked if the Germans were now willing to grant the Americans direct access to Curveball. The German station chief replied that meeting the source wasn't worthwhile, because Curveball was crazy. It would be a waste of time. The German told Drumheller that his service wasn't sure Curveball was telling the truth, and worse, that there were questions about his mental stability and reliability, particularly since he had suffered a nervous breakdown. The message was painfully clear: the Americans shouldn't use Curveball's information.

Drumheller passed on these warnings to top CIA managers, thinking that would be the end of Curveball's reporting. "I said it is going to make us look stupid if we don't validate this," Drumheller recalled.

Warnings Ignored

But Drumheller hadn't reckoned on the strength of the agency's embrace of Curveball and his pro-WMD intelligence. By January 2003, Drumheller was shocked to learn that Curveball's reporting was going to be included in Colin Powell's UN presentation, scheduled for early February.

One week before Powell made his presentation, Drumheller was shown a draft of his speech. It didn't mention Curveball or the Germans, but it did include assertions about the existence of Iraqi mobile bioweapons trailers that came straight from Curveball. Drumheller wasn't a technical bioweapons expert, but he did know about intelligence operations, and he knew that the tradecraft in the Curveball case was shoddy at best. Earlier in January, the German intelligence service had sent a cable to the CIA saying that the Americans could use Curveball's reporting in Powell's presentation—but also warning that it couldn't vouch for the information. Drumheller realized that he had to move fast to get this flawed material out of Powell's presentation, and so he called McLaughlin's assistant to set up an urgent meeting with the deputy CIA director.

At the start of the meeting, McLaughlin's executive assistant told the deputy director that Drumheller had serious problems with Curveball. McLaughlin responded in a way that surprised and troubled Drumheller.

"I hope not," McLaughlin said, according to Drumheller. "This is the heart of the case." The CIA's case that Iraq had a biological weapons program rested almost entirely on Curveball. Until that moment, Drumheller had no idea that the CIA had almost nothing else.

Drumheller quickly explained to McLaughlin how shaky the case was, and how there were concerns that Curveball might be a fabricator. As Drumheller left, McLaughlin told his assistant to "try to take care of this," and Drumheller once again felt confident that he had prevented a disaster.

"I thought they were going to drop it," Drumheller recalled. "I told the Germans they were going to drop it." Just to make sure, Drumheller's European Division sent a copy of Powell's draft speech back to top CIA managers with the Curveball material scratched out. . . .

[On February 6, 2003] Drumheller was at work at CIA headquarters when his wife called him. She was watching Powell's presentation on television and had called to tell him quickly to turn it on. To Drumheller's astonishment, he saw that Powell was making the forceful case for the existence of an Iraqi biological weapons program based on reports of mobile weapons labs. . . .

Hiding Doubts from the President

It is unclear whether these glaring gaps in the intelligence were ever clearly explained to President Bush. It is entirely possible that the doubts shared by many CIA officials about the quality of the intelligence on Iraqi WMD were kept away from the White House. If so, that self-censorship may have involved the most important document produced by the CIA—the President's Daily Brief [PDB], an exclusive report sent to the president each morning containing a summary of the day's most important intelligence. One senior former CIA official reports that frustrated CIA staffers came to him to tell him that there had been articles written for the President's Daily Brief that raised questions about the evidence concerning Iraqi WMD, but that those articles were removed from the PDB before it was sent to the White House. It has not been possible to confirm these claims with other sources. But it does not appear that the President's Daily Brief ever reflected the level of skepticism about the quality of the intelligence that was widespread within the CIA.

Of course, it is hard to say how Bush might have reacted if he had received a PDB that raised doubts about the existence of Iraq's weapons programs. He too might have ignored the warnings or even dismissed the articles. But it is also possible that he would have asked a few follow-up questions, which might then have forced the CIA to provide better supporting evidence for its many other reports that stated flatly that Iraq did have WMD programs. If someone had spoken up clearly and forcefully, the entire house of cards might have collapsed. A little bit of digging might have revealed the truth. A post-war investigation by the Senate Select Committee on Intelligence suggested that hard questions could have made a difference—most of the key judgments in the intelligence community's October 2002 National Intelligence Estimate, the Senate panel concluded, were either "overstated, or were not supported by the underlying intelligence reporting." The independent WMD commission went further, flatly stating that the intelligence community's prewar assessments about Iraq's weapons of mass destruction "were all wrong."

6

The CIA Did a Poor Job of Gathering Intelligence About WMDs in Iraq

Commission on the Intelligence Capabilities of the United States Regarding Weapons of Mass Destruction

On February 6, 2004, President George W. Bush launched the Commission on the Intelligence Capabilities of the United States Regarding Weapons of Mass Destruction. The commission's mission was to examine whether the Central Intelligence Agency (CIA) and other U.S. intelligence agencies had the capabilities that they needed in order to produce the necessary intelligence regarding the biological, chemical, and nuclear weapons capabilities of foreign countries and terrorist groups. The members of the commission included former governor of Virginia Charles S. Robb; Judge Laurence H. Silberman, of the U.S. Court of Appeals for the District of Columbia Circuit; Richard C. Levin, president of Yale University; Arizona senator John McCain; Hoover Institution fellow Henry S. Rowen; former undersecretary of defense for policy Walter B. Slocombe; Admiral William O. Studeman (Ret.), former deputy director of the CIA; Charles M. Vest, former president of the Massachusetts Institute of Technology; and Judge Patricia Wald, formerly of the U.S. Court of Appeals for the District of Colombia Circuit. On March 31, 2005, the commission submitted its report to the president; the following selection is an excerpt from that report.

Commission on the Intelligence Capabilities of the United States Regarding Weapons of Mass Destruction, *Report to the President of the United States*. Washington, DC: Government Printing Office, 2005, pp. 45–51.

The Central Intelligence Agency (CIA) and other U.S. intelligence agencies were almost entirely wrong in their assessments of Iraq's intention to build weapons of mass destruction (WMD) before the U.S. invasion in 2003. These intelligence failures stemmed from three major sources: a failure to collect sufficient intelligence about Iraq; a reliance on informants whose truthfulness was questionable or who were actually known to be liars; and a presumption that Iraq did have an active WMD program, regardless of evidence to the contrary.

As war loomed, the U.S. Intelligence Community was charged with telling policymakers what it knew about Iraq's nuclear, biological, and chemical weapons programs. The Community's best assessments were set out in an October 2002 National Intelligence Estimate, or NIE, a summation of the Community's views. The title, *Iraq's Continuing Programs for Weapons of Mass Destruction*, foretells the conclusion: that Iraq was still pursuing its programs for weapons of mass destruction (WMD). Specifically, the NIE assessed that Iraq had reconstituted its nuclear weapons program and could assemble a device by the end of the decade; that Iraq had biological weapons and mobile facilities for producing biological warfare (BW) agents; that Iraq had both renewed production of chemical weapons, and probably had chemical weapons stockpiles of up to 500 metric tons; and that Iraq was developing unmanned aerial vehicles (UAVs) probably intended to deliver BW agent.

These assessments were all wrong.

This became clear as U.S. forces searched without success for the WMD that the Intelligence Community had predicted. Extensive post-war investigations were carried out by the Iraq Survey Group (ISG). The ISG found no evidence that Iraq had tried to reconstitute its capability to produce nuclear weapons after 1991; no evidence of BW agent stockpiles or of mobile biological weapons production facilities; and no substantial chemical warfare (CW) stockpiles or credible indications that Baghdad [Iraq's capital] had resumed production of CW after 1991. Just about the only thing that the Intelligence Community got right was its pre-war conclusion that Iraq had deployed missiles with ranges exceeding United Nations limitations.

How could the Intelligence Community have been so mistaken? That is the question the President [George W. Bush] charged this Commission with answering. . . .

Intelligence Is Difficult Work

For commissions of this sort, 20/20 hindsight is an occupational hazard. It is easy to forget just how difficult a business intelligence is. Nations and terrorist groups do not easily part with their secrets—and they guard nothing more jealously than secrets related to nuclear, biological, and chemical weapons. Stealing those secrets, particularly from closed and repressive regimes like Saddam Hussein's Iraq, is no easy task, and failure is more common than success. Intelligence analysts will often be forced to make do with limited, ambiguous data: extrapolations from thin streams of information will be the norm.

The Intelligence Community could and should have come much closer to assessing the true state of Iraq's weapons programs than it did.

Indeed, defenders of the Intelligence Community have asked whether it would be fair to expect the Community to get the Iraq WMD question absolutely right. How, they ask, could our intelligence agencies have concluded that Saddam Hussein *did not* have weapons of mass destruction—given his history of using them, his previous deceptions, and his repeated efforts to obstruct United Nations inspectors? And after all, the United States was not alone in error; other major intelligence services also thought that Iraq had weapons of mass destruction.

We agree, but only in part. We do not fault the Intelligence Community for formulating the hypothesis, based on Saddam Hussein's conduct, that Iraq had retained an unconventional weapons capability and was working to augment this capability. Nor do we fault the Intelligence Community for failing to uncover what few Iraqis knew; according to the Iraq Survey Group only a handful of Saddam Hussein's closest advisors were aware of some of his decisions to halt work on his nuclear program and to destroy his stocks of chemical and biological weapons. Even if an extraordinary intelligence effort had gained access to one of these confidants, doubts would have lingered.

But with all that said, we conclude that the Intelligence Community could and should have come much closer to assessing the true state of Iraq's weapons programs than it did. It should have been less wrong—and, more importantly, it should have been more candid about what it did not know. In particular, it should have recognized the serious—and knowable—weaknesses in the evidence it accepted as providing hard confirmation that Iraq had retained WMD capabilities and programs.

Why Was the CIA so Wrong?

The Intelligence Community's errors were not the result of simple bad luck, or a once-in-a-lifetime "perfect storm," as some would have it. Rather, they were the product of poor intelligence collection, an analytical process that was driven by assumptions and inferences rather than data, inadequate validation and vetting of dubious intelligence sources, and numerous other breakdowns in the various processes that Intelligence Community professionals collectively describe as intelligence "tradecraft." In many ways, the Intelligence Community simply did not do the job that it exists to do.

Our review revealed failings at each stage of the intelligence process. Many past discussions of the Iraq intelligence failure have focused on intelligence analysis, and we indeed will have much to say about how analysts tackled the Iraq WMD question. But they could not analyze data that they did not have, so we begin by addressing the failure of the Intelligence Community to collect more useful intelligence in Iraq.

There is no question that collecting intelligence on Iraq's weapons programs was difficult. Saddam Hussein's regime had a robust and ruthless security system and engaged in sophisticated efforts to conceal or disguise its activities from outside intelligence services—efforts referred to within the Intelligence Community as "denial and deception." The United States had no Iraq embassy or official in-country presence; human intelligence operations were often conducted at a distance. And much of what we wanted to know was concealed in compartmented corners of the Iraqi regime to which few even at high levels in the Iraqi government had access.

Still, Iraq was a high-priority target for years, and the Intelligence Community should have done better. It collected precious little information about Iraq's weapons programs in the years before the Iraq war. And not only did the Community collect too little, but much of what it managed to collect had grave defects that should have been clear to analysts and policymakers at the time. Indeed, one of the most serious failures by the Intelligence Community was its failure to apply sufficiently rigorous tests to the evidence it collected. This failure touched all the most salient pieces of evidence relied on by our intelligence agencies, including the aluminum tubes, reporting on mobile BW, uranium from Niger, and assertions about UAVs.

Reliance on Bad Sources

One of the most painful errors, however, concerned Iraq's biological weapons programs. Virtually all of the Intelligence Community's information on Iraq's alleged mobile biological weapons facilities was supplied by a source, codenamed "Curveball," who was a fabricator. We discuss at length how Curve-ball came to play so prominent a role in the Intelligence Community's biological weapons assessments. It is, at bottom, a story of Defense Department collectors who abdicated their responsibility to vet a critical source; of Central Intelligence Agency (CIA) analysts who placed undue emphasis on the source's reporting because the tales he told were consistent with what they already believed; and, ultimately, of Intelligence Community leaders who failed to tell policymakers about Curveball's flaws in the weeks before war.

Curveball was not the only bad source the Intelligence Community used. Even more indefensibly, information from a source who was *already known* to be a fabricator found its way into finished pre-war intelligence products, including the October 2002 NIE. This intelligence was also allowed into Secretary of State Colin Powell's speech to the United Nations Security Council. despite the source having been officially discredited almost a year earlier. This communications breakdown could have been avoided if the Intelligence Community had a uniform requirement to reissue or recall reporting from a source whose information turns out to be fabricated, so that analysts do not continue to rely on an unreliable report. In the absence of such a system, however, the Defense Intelligence Agency (DIA), which disseminated the report in the first place, had a responsibility to make sure that its bad source did not continue to pollute policy judgments; DIA did not fulfill this obligation.

Presuming Iraq Was Guilty

Lacking reliable data about Iraq's programs, analysts' starting point was Iraq's history—its past use of chemical weapons, its successful concealment of WMD programs both before and after the Gulf War, and its failure to account for previously declared stockpiles. The analysts' operating hypothesis, therefore, was that Iraq probably still possessed hidden chemical and biological weapons, was still seeking to rebuild its nuclear weapons program, and was seeking to increase its capability to produce and deliver chemical and biological weapons. This hypothesis was not unreasonable; the problem was that, over time, it hardened into a presumption. This hard and fast presumption then contributed to analysts' readiness to accept pieces of evidence that, even at the time, they should have seen as seriously flawed.

In essence, analysts shifted the burden of proof, requiring evidence that Iraq did *not* have WMD. More troubling, some analysts started to disregard evidence that did not support their premise. Chastened by the effectiveness of Iraq's deceptions before the Gulf War, they viewed contradictory information not as evidence that their premise might be mistaken, but as evidence that Iraq was continuing to conceal its weapons programs.

The Intelligence Community's analysis of the high-strength aluminum tubes offers an illustration of these problems. Most agencies in the Intelligence Community assessed—incorrectly—that these were intended for use in a uranium enrichment program. The reasoning that supported this position was, first, that the tubes *could* be used in centrifuges and, second, that Iraq was good at hiding its nuclear program.

By focusing on whether the tubes could be used for centrifuges, analysts effectively set aside evidence that the tubes were better suited for use in rockets, such as the fact that the tubes had precisely the same dimensions and were made of the same material as tubes used in the conventional rockets that Iraq had declared to international inspectors in 1996. And Iraq's denial and deception capabilities allowed analysts to find support for their view even from information that seemed to contradict it. Thus, Iraqi claims that the tubes were for rockets were described as an Iraqi "cover story" designed to conceal the nuclear end-use for the tubes. In short, analysts erected a theory that almost could not be disproved—both confirming and contradictory facts were construed as support for the theory that the tubes were destined for use in centrifuges.

It was the paucity of intelligence and poor analytical tradecraft, rather than political pressure, that produced the inaccurate pre-war intelligence assessments.

Keeping Secrets from Policymakers

In the absence of direct evidence, premises and inferences must do. Analysts cannot be faulted for failures of collection. But they can be faulted for not telling policymakers just how little evidence they had to back up their inferences and how uncertain even that evidence itself was. The October 2002 NIE and other pre-war intelligence assessments failed to articulate the thinness of the intelligence upon which critical judgments about Iraq's weapons programs hinged.

Our study also revealed deficiencies in particular intelligence products that are used to convey intelligence information to senior policymakers. As noted above, during the course of its investigation the Commission reviewed a number of articles from the President's Daily Brief (PDB) relating to Iraq's WMD programs. Not surprisingly, many of the flaws in other intelligence products can also be found in the PDBs. But we found some flaws that were inherent in the format of the PDBs—a series of short "articles" often based on current intelligence reporting that are presented to the President each morning. Their brevity leaves little room for doubts or nuance—and their "headlines" designed to grab the reader's attention leave no room at all. Also, a daily drumbeat of reports on the same topic gives an impression of confirming evidence, even when the reports all come from the same source.

The Commission also learned that, on the eve of war, the Intelligence Community failed to convey important information to policymakers. After the October 2002 NIE was published, but before Secretary of State Powell made his address about Iraq's WMD programs to the United Nations, serious doubts became known within the Intelligence Community about Curveball, the aforementioned human intelligence source whose reporting was so critical to the Intelligence Community's pre-war biological warfare assessments. These doubts never found their way to Secretary Powell, who was at that time attempting to strip questionable information from his speech.

These are errors—serious errors. But these errors stem from poor tradecraft and poor management. The Commission found no evidence of polilical pressure to influence the Intelligence Community's pre-war assessments of Iraq's weapons programs. . . . Analysts universally asserted that in no instance did political pressure cause them to skew or alter any of their analytical judgments. We conclude that it was the paucity of intelligence and poor analytical tradecraft, rather than political pressure, that produced the inaccurate pre-war intelligence assessments.

7

The American Intelligence System Needs Serious Reform

Economist

The Economist *is a weekly Bristish newspaper.*

Few people argue with the idea that America's intelligence system needs serious reform. The Intelligence Reform and Terrorism Prevention Act of 2004 made many changes, including separating the jobs of director of the Central Intelligence Agency (CIA) and director of national intelligence and creating a National Counterterrorism Center that is separate from the existing fifteen intelligence agencies. It is unclear, however, if those changes will be enough to overcome the extensive problems in the way that intelligence is gathered and analyzed in the United States.

"We tend to meet any new situation in life by reorganising," Petronius Arbiter, a 1st-century Roman satirist, is supposed to have remarked. "And what a wonderful method it can be for creating the illusion of progress while producing confusion, inefficiency and demoralisation." Wonderful, indeed, for John Negroponte, America's ambassador to Iraq, who will leave Baghdad [Iraq] [March 2005] to become America's first director of national intelligence (DNI). Mr. Negroponte may come to question which job is the more harrowing. On one side, murder and mayhem; on the other, mayhem and mystery.

The creation of the DNI was a well publicised reform, approved by both Republicans and Democrats, which was intended to improve the performance of America's intelligence agencies in the wake of the terrorist attacks of September 11th 2001. But precisely what power it will confer on Mr. Negroponte is, as yet, unknown. So too is what power he will subtract from others within the 15 arcane agencies he will direct. The Central Intelligence Agency (CIA), the best known, accounts for only about a tenth of the intelligence budget; the biggest of all, the National Security Agency (NSA), with 30,000 employees resides in the Department of Defence (DOD) under the pugnacious [Secretary of Defense] Donald Rumsfeld. As Mr. Negroponte turns his thoughts away from bombs and gunfire inside the green zone, he may hear a rattle of daggers being drawn in Washington, Arlington [headquarters of the DOD] and Langley [headquarters of the CIA].

Intelligence Failures

America's secret world is inefficient and demoralised, and has been for some time. The CIA in particular is an unreformed, substantially unaccountable bureaucracy, which has almost never sacked anyone, which appears deluded by its own mythology and which, despite some notable successes, is burdened by a miserable run of failures. The entrance-hall at Langley is decorated with a black star for every CIA officer killed fighting the cold war. A more telling record, according to several former spooks, is that the agency in those years did not recruit a single mid-level or high-level Soviet agent. Every significant CIA informant was a volunteer. And the agency was comprehensively infiltrated. At one point, every CIA case-officer working on Cuba was a double agent. All but three CIA officers working on East Germany allegedly worked for the Stasi [East Germany's Ministry for State Security]. As for those brave volunteer agents, Aldrich Ames, a greedy drunkard in the CIA directorate of operations who was bought by the Russians, put paid to many—as did another mole, Robert Hanssen, in the FBI [Federal Bureau of Investigation].

When it comes to recruitment and filing intelligence from the field, quantity has often mattered most. In cold-war Africa, American spooks allegedly paid for the same information obtained for nothing by American diplomats over lunch. One recent case-officer, Lindsay Moran, says she was aware that an agent she was running in the Balkans was peddling worthless information, but she was repeatedly refused permission to end the contact. "It gets depressing," she said. "You start to wonder whether we can do anything good at all."

Left-wingers loathe the CIA . . . for its cold-war habit of plotting to murder left-wing leaders, including Patrice Lumumba of Congo and Fidel Castro of Cuba.

More recent events have brought shame on the intelligence agencies as a whole. They failed to predict both the Soviet invasion of Afghanistan in 1979 and the Soviet Union's break-up a decade later. In 1998, America's spies were taken by surprise when India tested a nuclear bomb; they then advised Bill Clinton to flatten one of Sudan's few medicine factories, wrongly believing that it made nerve gas. The next year, on the agencies' mistaken advice, an American warplane bombed China's embassy in Belgrade [Serbia].

The two main prompts to reform, however, have been the September 11th attacks, in which some 3,000 Americans died, and the spooks' hallucinations about Iraq's weapons programmes, which were used to justify a war and bloody peace that have cost tens of thousands of lives. The fallout from Iraq—especially a report by the Senate Intelligence Committee last year, which accused the agencies of "a lack of information-sharing, poor management, and inadequate intelligence collection"—forced George Tenet, the CIA's second-longest-serving boss, to resign in June [2004].

Leadership Problems

Under Mr Tenet's successor, Porter Goss, a former Republican congressman and spy, a dozen senior spooks have been sacked and two dozen have quit in fury. Mr. Goss's aides—most of whom have had no previous experience of intelligence work—are said to be thuggish managers. Mr. Goss is meanwhile finding his job tough. On March 2nd [2005], he said he was "a little amazed at the workload", which was "too much for this mortal". Merely preparing the president's daily intelligence briefing takes him five hours.

It was partly to ease this burden that the DNI was created, in a package of reforms passed in December [2004]. These were broadly in line with recommendations made by the bi-partisan 9/11 Commission, whose vivid report into the attacks was a deserved, if unlikely, bestseller last year [2004]. (The recommendations were not informed by the foul-up on Iraq; a presidential commission into the pre-war Iraq intelligence is due to report later this month [March 2005].)

The DNI will be charged with co-ordinating all the secret agencies, a job which the CIA's chief—as the director of central intelligence—has performed only in theory hitherto. The DNI will thus be held accountable for the performance of each agency. Alongside a new multi-agency National Counter-terrorism Centre (NCTC)—which will have wider powers than its existing equivalent, and may be the prototype for more specialist centres, focused on China and proliferation issues—the DNI represents the biggest organisational change to America's spy world since 1947.

Pre-9/11 Failures

The 9/11 Commission's report told mostly the story of the months and moments leading up to the attacks, with many details of the agencies' bungling. The CIA noticed that two known terrorists had obtained American visas, but failed to inform the Federal Bureau of Investigation, which is responsible for domestic counter-terrorism. Notoriously, certain FBI bosses failed to pick up on a report that a group of Arab men was learning to fly planes, but not to land them. Overall, the commissioners diagnosed a grave reluctance to share information within and among the agencies. Most seriously, they found that the FBI's two main departments, responsible for intelligence and criminal investigations, barely communicated. In part, they were deterred by laws safeguarding Americans from government meddling, though the reach of these laws was often exaggerated.

Nobody really disputes the idea that America's intelligence system, which was designed in 1947, was out of date, disorganised and had no recognisable chief.

More generally, the commission observed a "failure of imagination" in the agencies' response to the warning signs they did observe. A CIA report filed in 1998 had warned that al-Qaeda might carry out suicide attacks with hijacked planes; but the report's authors later said they could barely remember having included the detail. The problems were only partly organisational. Indeed, the commission noted that, when tipped off that al-Qaeda was planning a range of horrific attacks to mark the end of the last millennium, the agencies performed well; a number of bomb attacks on embassies in the Middle East were averted.

The commission proposed that a DNI, crudely analogous to the head of the armed forces, the chairman of the joint chiefs of staff, should be hired to oversee all the agencies and correct what had gone wrong. To lend weight to his admonishments, the DNI was to be given charge of the agencies' combined $40 billion budget, though most of that is controlled by the Pentagon. The DNI would be just what the agencies had not been: vigilant, imaginative and single-minded.

Post-9/11 Changes

Nobody really disputes the idea that America's intelligence system, which was designed in 1947, was out of date, disorganised and had no recognisable chief. Its 15 squabbling baronies, which were set up to deal with conventional enemies, display precious little cohesion (with the Pentagon particularly protective of the agencies it controls). It was thus not surprising that the 9/11 commissioners fastened on the idea of appointing an overall chief to bring the muddle together. The question is whether this new job, without any other structural reform, can actually improve the system.

By the time the commission delivered its recommendations, some of the more useful ones were almost three years out of date. The commission's period under investigation ended on September 11th 2001; the commission's report was delivered 34 months later. In the intervening time, the war on terror was launched and changes were made. First, under the Patriot Act, many of the inter-agency firewalls protecting Americans' civil liberties were broken down. FBI and other agents were obliged to share intelligence on terrorists within and among the agencies. The director of the FBI, Robert Mueller, was required to attend the president's daily intelligence briefing, given by the director of central intelligence (DCI).

Huge resources were shifted to counter-terrorism. In January 2003, multi-agency counter-terrorism think-tank, the Terrorist Threat Integration Centre, was formed inside the CIA's headquarters. The centre produces a daily briefing on terrorist threats and counter-terrorism operations, which the president hears after the DCI's.

Intelligence Reform and Terrorism Prevention Act

When the 9/11 Commission added its own recommendations to the pile, they were accepted rapidly. John Kerry, the Democratic presidential candidate, endorsed the report almost before he could have read it. Bereaved relatives of the hijackers' victims rallied behind its recommendations. Reluctantly, and to Mr. Rumsfeld's great annoyance, Mr. Bush endorsed it too.

On the right, the CIA is often considered a nest of liberals, bureaucratic and broken beyond repair, whose salvageable assets should be handed over to the Pentagon.

To general surprise, Mr. [George W.] Bush after his re-election made good on that endorsement, signing into law the Intelligence Reform and Terrorism Prevention Act. It was modelled on the commission's recommendations, with a few modifications insisted on by pals of Mr. Rumsfeld. For example, in keeping with the commission's demands, the act authorises the DNI to "design and deliver" a unified intelligence budget. But it also says that the authority of the cabinet secretaries should be upheld.

This has created confusion over who will, in fact, control the purse-strings. To extricate the defence intelligence budgets from the wider defence budget could take several years and a staff of several hundred experts. It might not even be desirable. America's generals almost always get first dibs on the intelligence assets, such as spy satellites, that they share with civilian agencies, and in wartime they always do. The law similarly gives the DNI control over the agencies' personnel, but here too there is devilment in the detail: in practice, the DNI can veto the appointment of some second-tier officials, but he will not be able to sack agency chiefs.

To shore up the DNI's putative powers, Mr. Bush has suggested that Mr. Negroponte, not Mr. Goss, will deliver his morning intelligence briefing. In theory, this should allow Mr. Goss to concentrate on managing the CIA. In practice, the briefing is likely still to be prepared by the CIA and Mr. Goss will still be required to attend the meetings, with Mr. Negroponte appearing as an over-qualified court herald. Alternatively, he too could spend half his working day drafting the briefing. He will exert even less control over what goes into the counter-terrorism briefing that follows it, because although the DNI will be in overall charge of the NCTC, the agency chiefs retain control of their operations. Yet Mr. Negroponte is to be held accountable for their mistakes.

Debate Over Reform

These uncertainties have fuelled a noisy and ill-tempered debate about the reforms in a country whose spies have traditionally excited fierce passions, and where national security is a national obsession. Left-wingers loathe the CIA, in particular, or its cold-war habit of plotting to murder left-wing leaders, including Patrice Lumumba of Congo and Fidel Castro of Cuba. On the right, the CIA is often considered a nest of liberals, bureaucratic and broken beyond repair, whose salvageable assets should be handed over to the Pentagon. Some hawks justify the policy of pre-emption on the ground that the agencies cannot be trusted to give warning of imminent threats. And, of course, moderate opponents of all the above tend to take the opposite view.

Such passions lie behind the unerring certainty with which America's politicians and pundits speak of a world that remains, after all, secret. For many right-wingers, the DNI office will prove disastrous, adding an unwanted layer of bureaucracy to an already constipated system. At worst, it will go the way of the Office of Homeland Security, which was created after the September 11th attacks with a mandate to co-ordinate agencies such as customs and the coast guard, but which has since proved toothless and wasteful. Others note the few factors in Mr. Negroponte's favour. His chosen deputy, Lieut[enant]-General Michael Hayden, is a well-respected former head of the NSA. Above all, Mr. Negroponte will have daily access to a president who holds him in high regard.

The truth is, no one knows how the reforms will proceed. Mr. Negroponte may gain a modicum of control over the agencies. At best, he may ensure that the information channels opened within and between the agencies after the hijack attacks stay open. Yet, on his own at least, he will not be able to fix the agencies' most grievous problems, highlighted by their performance on Iraq.

Bad Intelligence on Iraq

Last year [2004] Senate report into the Iraq debacle found America's spies—and especially the CIA—negligent and incompetent at every stage of the intelligence-collection and analysis process. The CIA had not a single agent in Iraq after the UN's [United Nations] weapons inspectors were expelled in 1998. They had no flesh intelligence to claim, as they did, that Iraq had chemical and biological weapons. Their claim that Iraq was "reconstituting its nuclear programme" was based on the country's import of some aluminium tubes that could have been used for other purposes, and was fiercely contested by most experts across the agencies. They did not, at least, suggest that Iraq was in cahoots with al-Qaeda, although members of the government, notably Dick Cheney, the vice-president, did so often.

The key to the agencies' misapprehensions, the committee found, was a predilection to "group-think". In other words, they failed to re-examine received truths—for example, the historical fact that Iraq had prohibited weapons. This was made manifest in numerous ways. The CIA's analysis was seldom double-checked; detection of dual-purpose materials, that might possibly be used in weapon programmes, was routinely taken as proof that such programmes existed; and ambiguous scraps of intelligence were compiled to reach an unambiguous conclusion, a process known as "layering". These problems, said the report, stemmed "from a broken corporate culture and poor management, and will not be solved by additional funding and personnel."

The spies' friends (and Mr. Bush's enemies) rebut this. On chemical and biological weapons, they say, the agencies were not all that wrong—the report acknowledged that Iraq had retained the technology to rebuild its stockpiles—and, moreover, no other western intelligence service thought differently. On Iraq's nuclear programme, they say, the government was to blame: under intense pressure to provide the case for a war that Mr. Bush had already decided to fight, doubters were muffled and caveats were cut.

America's spies do not necessarily need shifting; a good few need sacking.

Another defence is that intelligence, whether human or, far more commonly, electronic, rarely yields the smoking-gun proofs that policymakers may wish for. It is an accumulation of indicators, contradictory and unreliable, which intelligence analysts turn into an estimation of a hidden reality—or, even more precariously, use to predict the future. Intelligence is inherently faulty. True: but why then did Mr. Tenet—in a phrase quoted by Bob Woodward, which Mr. Tenet has not disputed—describe the case for Iraq having banned weapons as "a slam-dunk"?

Deeper Reform Needed

Despite all the recommendations, the rot may be hard to stop. After a decade of cuts—the CIA's budget was chopped by 23% under [former president] Bill Clinton—the agencies are indeed getting more money and more spies. This year [2005], the CIA will graduate its biggest-ever class of case-officers. With only around 1,200 stationed overseas, more case-officers are needed, but only if they are properly equipped for the latest challenges. Around half of all the CIA's case-officers are in

Baghdad. But with only a handful of them fluent in Arabic, they are mostly confined to the green zone, condemned to interview Iraqi interpreters and watch endless episodes of [the TV show] "Sex and the City" on DVD.

Further organisational reform would not eliminate the problem. America's spies do not necessarily need shifting; a good few need sacking. Mr. Negroponte is in too lofty and exposed a seat to manage such a programme. But if he can shoulder some of the DCI's more onerous duties, including the president's briefing and the intelligence budget, he might free a dynamic CIA director to wield the axe for him. There is no time to waste. In a precarious world, the full range of American intelligence and intelligence-gathering on, for example, China's military build-up and Iran's nuclear ambitions needs urgent re-evaluating. But that dynamic director may not be Mr. Goss, who sounds awfully tired.

8

The CIA Should Change the Way It Analyzes Intelligence

Gary J. Schmitt

Gary J. Schmitt is a resident fellow at the American Enterprise Institute, a conservative think tank in Washington, D.C. He is also the coauthor, with Abram N. Shulsky, of the book Silent Warfare: Understanding the World of Intelligence.

The intelligence community has historically thought that its most important job is to produce long-range estimates of the future intentions and capabilities of America's enemies. In order to keep these estimates unbiased, the intelligence community has also agreed that there needs to be a strict separation between itself and the policy makers who use the information that it provides. However, it is not clear that this emphasis on producing impartial long-range estimates actually leads to the creation of intelligence that is useful to policy makers. The Central Intelligence Agency and other intelligence agencies could better fulfill their core mission of providing useful information to the people who make decisions about American foreign policy by cooperating more closely with those policy makers to analyze current events and the potential American responses to them.

The 9/11 Commission's final report has surprising little to say about the craft of intelligence analysis. Out of nearly five hundred pages, probably no more than a half dozen are directly concerned with analysis. Given the major overhauls in

Berkowitz, Peter, ed., *The Future of American Intelligence*, Stanford, CA: Hoover Institution Press, 2005. Copyright © 2005 by the Board of Trustees of the Leland Stanford Junior University. Reprinted by permission of Hoover Institution Press.

the intelligence community proposed by the Commission and then enacted into law, the absence of an extended discussion about analysis is striking. It is all the more conspicuous because so much of the literature on surprise attacks (and on surprises more generally) focuses on the analytic failures leading up to the events in question. Why weren't "the dots" connected? How was the enemy able to deceive and mislead its opponent? What was the character of the particular myopia [short-sightedness] or methodological flaws that kept people in the dark until too late?

The Commission's report does not provide answers to these questions.

Nevertheless, the Commission does make one very large point about intelligence analysis that is important to note—and to examine. According to the Commission, the core analytic failure was one of a lack of "imagination." As commissioner and former secretary of the Navy John Lehman remarked: When the Commission studied the government's "documents, the internal papers, the recommendations of the top advisers to presidents, we were shocked at the failure to grasp the extent of [the] evil that was stalking us." Put simply, the government had not come to grips with the novelty and the gravity of the threat posed by Osama bin Laden. And it was the intelligence community's analysts—distracted by, and pulled in the direction of providing current intelligence for, an ever-expanding array of priorities—who failed to undertake the kind of strategic big-think assessment of al Qaeda that might have shaken the government from its bureaucratic and political lethargy.

Intelligence About al Qaeda

According to the Commission, prior to 9/11, the U.S. intelligence community had not issued a new national intelligence estimate (NIE)—the most prestigious and most authoritative analytic product of the whole intelligence community—on terrorism since 1995. And though the 1995 NIE had predicted future terrorist attacks against the United States, including in the United States, other than a perfunctory 1997 "update," the intelligence community did not produce any authoritative accounts of bin Laden, his organization, or the threat he posed to the country. In some measure, the Commission argued this was part and parcel of "the conventional wisdom before 9/11" with respect to the threat posed by bin Laden: He was undoubtedly dangerous, but he was nothing "radically new, posing a threat beyond any yet experienced." For those inside government who thought differently, they needed some way to "at least spotlight the areas of dispute" and, potentially, generate new policies. In the past, according to the report, an NIE "has often played this role, and is sometimes controversial for this very reason." Indeed, "such assessments, which provoke widespread thought and debate, have a major impact on their recipients, often in a wider circle of decisionmakers." Yet, as already noted, there were no new NIEs, and, hence, by the Commission's lights, the intelligence community missed a critical opportunity to challenge the prevailing perception of the security problem posed by bin Laden and al Qaeda.

The opportunity was missed, the report suggests, because with the end of the Cold War, the lack of clarity about who America's real long-term enemies were, and what our long-term policy goals would be, undermined the intelligence community's ability to plow resources into "long-term accumulation of intellectual capital" on any given topic. Whatever else the Cold War had brought, it "had at least one positive effect: [I]t created an environment in which managers and analysts could safely invest time and resources in basic research, detailed and reflective." Within the analytic community. "a university culture with its version of books and articles was giving way to the culture of the newsroom."

Complaints about this trend in intelligence analysis are long standing, as is the implicit suggestion that the gold standard when it comes to analysis is the dispassionate approach of the university scholar. What the government needs, in this view, is less its own in-house CNN than, in the words of one former House intelligence committee chair, an analytic arm that is the equivalent of "a world-class 'think tank.'". . .

Although objectivity should remain a goal for analysts, there is, unfortunately, no institutional arrangement that can guarantee it.

Current Analysis

What then are the implications for the tradecraft of analysis and the relationship between policy and intelligence if we rethink the existing paradigm?

The first thing, perhaps, is to stop thinking of current intelligence analysis as the ugly stepsister to the more edifying work of producing long-range estimates. But such thinking has a strong hold on Washington's mind. From the Church Committee of the 1970s [that investigated the Watergate affair] to the panel investigating the intelligence community's failure to foresee the nuclear weapons tests by Pakistan in 1998 to the 9/11 Commission, the complaint has been that the job of providing current intelligence keeps getting in the way of providing high-quality estimates that give policy makers the kind of warning necessary to avoid strategic surprises. But is the trade-off between the resources and attention devoted to current intelligence versus those given to producing longer-term analysis really the problem? Or is the actual problem the unrealistic expectations about what predictive capacities estimates can have? If so, should the failures of the latter really be laid at the feet of the former? And, if not, shouldn't we accept the fact that policy makers have always wanted, and will continue to want, to be kept abreast of the latest information? Hence, isn't it the analytic community's job to make sure policy makers get the information they want, need, and, at times, have not asked for?

That said, the intelligence community also has to avoid falling into the trap of trying to become the government's CNN. If it is unrealistic for policy makers to expect analysts to predict the future reliably, it is equally unrealistic for policy makers to expect the intelligence community not to get "scooped" by the CNNs of the world. Policy makers might not like seeing events on their office television first or reading about them initially on the Internet, but the fact is, the intelligence community is not really equipped, in terms of global coverage and instantaneous reporting, to compete with the news media. Nor is it clear that it should be.

The intelligence community has a comparative advantage over the media in the area of current intelligence. The intelligence community is able to comment on the reporting as it is received—placing it in context and assessing the reliability of initial reports—and, in turn, to target collection assets to collect additional information that rounds out (or contradicts) the picture being conveyed by the international media. However, neither of these functions can be done instantaneously; during the interim, the CNNs of the world and the Internet will be the principal game in town.

Intelligence and Policy Decisions

One practical step the intelligence community could take in the face of these realities is to provide senior policy makers with "information specialists." The information specialist would sort through the avalanche of information, spot important items for the policy maker, and be the day-to-day conduit to the intelligence agencies, asking for and receiving from them the required additional data necessary to help fill out a particular picture. Precisely because such specialists come from the intelligence community, they will have better access to specialized intelligence sources and methods, and hence, they will be in a better position to fuse intelligence information with other sources.

To carry out this function effectively, the intelligence officer assigned to this role will inevitably be knee-deep in the workings of the policy shop. He or she will have to know what the government's policies are, what policy options are under consideration, what the adversary is like, and, to some degree, what our own diplomatic and military capabilities might be. Like a scout who goes to watch next week's opponent and reports back to the head coach, the best scouts will have in the back of their mind what their own team's plans and capabilities are so they can properly assess the particular strengths and weaknesses of the other team. The "matchups" are as important as an abstract description of what plays and defenses the other team tends to run. But this means tearing down the "sacred curtain" between intelligence and policy making that still defines so much of our discussions about the relationship. It also requires returning to an older conception of the relationship found, for example, in the role of the G-2 [assistant chief of staff for intelligence] on a military commander's staff. Here, an officer, trained as an intelligence official but under the commander's charge, is charged with collating, analyzing, and briefing all the information coming in to the staff. And precisely because he works on the staff, he will be more familiar with operational plans and his commander's priorities. This, in turn, should give him a better idea of both what to ask for from intelligence and what new intelligence is most likely to have a significant impact on the plans themselves.

Avoiding Surprises

A second implication of this rethinking about the analytic function and its relationship to policy relates to the intelligence community's indications and warning (I&W) function. Put simply, during the Cold War, U.S. intelligence—fearing a nuclear Pearl Harbor—fashioned an extensive and expensive I&W system. This was one surprise no one wanted to face. As best can be seen from publicly available literature, the system seems to have worked well enough when it came to that one issue. Of course, no one knows for sure, because we don't know of one instance where planning for a strategic intercontinental exchange was actually in the works. But what we do know is that we have been surprised sufficiently often enough that the desire to avoid it appears to be more a hope than something to be counted on.

However, precisely because avoiding surprise was ... so important ... the tendency has been to look at this issue as though one were a college professor grading an exam consisting of only one true/false question. Were we surprised? If the answer is "yes," then the intelligence community has failed. If the answer is "no," then it has passed. Naturally enough, the bureaucratic response to such a grading system has often been to hide warnings about potential adverse events in a sea of qualifiers or behind obscure language. If nothing happens, senior policy makers will not likely have noticed or cared enough to revisit what they were told; if something does happen, the intelligence bureaucracy will quickly point to that sentence or two—abstracted from the rest of the analysis—that shows they were on top of things.

To end this self-defeating cycle, the analysts and their policy customers have to lower their sights. While the intelligence community should, when it can, tip off policy makers to unexpected events, its principal focus should be less avoiding surprises and more conveying warnings. The goal should be to give policy makers a head's up about those things they should worry about and should possibly take action to head off. Preoccupied senior officials will also need to be given some idea of whether they will likely get any further notice of what might take place before it happens. Again, the measure of effectiveness should not be "Were we surprised?" but "Were we at the appropriate level of readiness?" Policy makers, of course, will complain that this approach might lead to an equally daunting set of problems brought about by a "Chicken Little" syndrome on the part of analysts. Perhaps. But anything that makes policy makers more deliberative is to be preferred to a system that creates incentives for just the opposite.

Finally, if the goal of the I&W system is not to avoid surprise but to warn policy makers of potential dangers in order to spur policy deliberation, it follows that analysts should also consider part of the I&W function to include alerting policy makers of potential opportunities for taking advantageous action. This would require, of course, that analysts be sufficiently close to the policy process to understand policy objectives. As will be explained in the discussion of national intelligence estimates, this could be accomplished by closer contacts through the creation of joint policy-intelligence working groups on specific topics.

Competitive Intelligence Analysis

A national intelligence estimate is customarily thought to be the most prestigious, most authoritative, most comprehensive, most fully "processed" product of the American intelligence community. It is considered to be the "peak" of the analytic function. NIEs seek nothing less than to explain to policy makers some particular situation of importance by analyzing all the relevant dimensions, assessing the forces at work, and providing some forecast as to how the situation will evolve.

To do so, NIEs must be based on all available relevant data—whether it comes from open sources, clandestine collection, or diplomatic channels—and should be as objective as possible. In other words, an estimate should not reach conclusions designed to promote a given policy or to serve some bureaucratic interest of either its consumers or, for that matter, its producers. Traditionally, this has meant estimates as products of a centralized effort, working under the aegis of the Director of Central Intelligence, who, as the head of the intelligence community, is beholden neither to a policy-making department nor to a particular agency within the intelligence community.

However, these traditional rationales are not nearly as persuasive as they once were. Initially, a centralized effort was thought necessary to solve the so-called Pearl Harbor problem. Without a centralized effort to bring together all incoming intelligence, the likelihood of being surprised would go way up. Yet, in this day and age of computer-supported data banks and networked systems, it is no longer clear that "all-source" analysis for estimates need be done by one entity—be it one team or one agency. And, as already noted, the current estimating system cannot guarantee objectivity. Although objectivity should remain a goal for analysts, there is, unfortunately, no institutional arrangement that can guarantee it.

> *What competing estimates can do . . . is force both analysts and policy makers to confront the hidden assumptions driving their own judgments.*

Moreover, objectivity is not something to be valued in and of itself. The reason we want objective analysis is to provide policy makers with the best information possible upon which they can base their decisions. Thus, the goal should be to make policy makers more deliberative and not give them the pseudocomfort (or, at times, discomfort) that comes from an estimate that typically reflects the conventional wisdom on a given topic. Because every intelligence agency has to work for somebody ultimately, an alternative approach is an increased use of competitive analysis for estimates—that is, a system through which various analytic centers, working for different bosses, develop their own views on the same topic. At a minimum, the resulting debate should make it more difficult for agencies to "cook" their assessments and would alert policy makers to a range of possibilities, which would, it is hoped, sharpen their own thinking.

The downside usually tied to this suggestion is that a policy maker will pick the analysis that fits his or her existing predilections. Yet given the speculative nature of many estimates in any case, there is no reason an experienced senior policy maker will not feel justified in trusting his or her own judgment, regardless of whether he or she is faced with one consensus-driven assessment or multiple competing ones. In short, having one "authoritative" estimate will not fix that problem. What competing estimates can do if written with rigor and lucidity in the handling of evidence, is force both analysts and policy makers to confront the hidden assumptions driving their own judgments. It doesn't guarantee a wise decision, but it may make the decision more informed. As one longtime senior policy maker remarked: "Policy makers are like surgeons. They don't last long if they ignore what they see when they cut an issue open.". . .

On the whole, the old . . . model for producing estimates, in which intelligence provides input to the policy process from afar, appears too simplistic. Moreover, by aping the natural sciences—that is, by passively looking at the world as though under some microscope—the approach taken by the intelligence community ignores a critical fact of international life today: U.S. behavior. If an estimate is to take into account all relevant aspects of a given issue or situation, what Washington does or doesn't do in any given situation will bear substantially on forecasts of what to expect. To take one old example, the question of whether the regime of the Shah of Iran would fall in the 1970s did not simply depend on what was going on inside Iran. Of no small importance was what the United States might do (or not do) in reaction to the political challenge the Shah faced. Yet, given the wall that is designed to separate intelligence from policy making, factoring in possible various U.S. policy decisions was not thought to be part of the intelligence community's writ. Given the unique superpower status the United States enjoys today, one might expect this problem to have grown more salient, not less.

Addressing this problem probably requires modifying the estimating process so that it becomes an interactive one between the intelligence and the policy-making communities. . . . Estimates could, when appropriate, more fully consider U.S. capabilities and options. This would highlight the importance of making the estimators aware of what Washington might be doing overtly or covertly with respect to any given situation and taking that into account. In this connection, estimates could make use of new formats and methods: for example, "net assessments," which explicitly compare American and competitors' capabilities and strategies, or "red teaming," which would analyze potential strategies that might be used by an adversary to thwart U.S. policies.

Finally, adopting this perspective would bring a healthy dose of reality to what estimates, in fact, involve—that is, a great deal of speculative judgment that cannot be reduced to professional, nonpolitical expertise. Intelligence analysts would retain certain advantages, not the least of which is the time to pull together all available information on a particular issue and examine it with rigor. But as important as this advantage may be, it is not a compelling reason to believe that the expertise and insights of policy makers, diplomats, or defense officials should be excluded when it comes to producing a national assessment on some topic. Indeed, one of the little-noted findings of the recent Senate Intelligence Committee, in its report on prewar assessments of Iraq's WMD [weapons of mass destruction] programs and its ties to terrorism, was that "probing questions" on the part of [George W.] Bush administration officials with respect to the issue of Iraq's ties to terrorism "actually improved the Central Intelligence Agency's (CIA) products."

9

The CIA Should Reform
Its Clandestine Service

Reuel Marc Gerecht

Reuel Marc Gerecht was formerly a specialist on the Middle East for the Central Intelligence Agency. He is now a resident fellow at the American Enterprise Institute.

Central Intelligence Agency (CIA) case officers, who work under-cover in foreign countries, are poorly positioned to gather intelligence on terrorist threats against the United States. Most of these case officers pose as employees at American embassies or as American businesspeople, but neither of these cover stories is useful in infiltrating terrorist groups. The CIA needs to hire more agents who can pass as Islamic militants and can move more easily inside terrorist circles.

Will [CIA director] Porter Goss reform the CIA's clandestine service? Though the media have focused on senior-level resignations under the new director, Goss's hiring priorities are a better indicator of whether meaningful change is arriving at Langley [Virginia, CIA headquarters]. So far, all signs show that his CIA will be the CIA of his predecessor: bureaucratically moribund at headquarters and operationally ineffectual in the field. If this were not the case, we would see Goss and the White House announcing plans first to fire, not hire, hundreds of operatives who do not advance the agency's primary counterterrorism mission.

Washington Post, February 1, 2005. Republished with permission of Reuel Marc Gerecht, conveyed through Copyright Clearance Center, Inc.

Inside Officers and NOCs

President [George W.] Bush, partly in response to the Sept. 11 commission's recommendations, has ordered the case officer cadre increased by 50 percent, augmenting the numbers both of "inside" officers, who usually work out of embassies and consulates, and, more important, the nonofficial cover officers, known inside the agency as NOCs (pronounced "knocks"). Since the CIA's beginning in 1947, "inside" officers have dominated the operations directorate. Even in the agency's most muscular years—the 1950s and the 1980s—nonofficial cover operatives represented only a tiny slice of the clandestine service.

According to active-duty CIA officers, there is a general realization that the number of nonofficial operatives needs to go up: It's difficult even to imagine scenarios in which the CIA's fake diplomats—the people under official cover—can meet, let alone "develop" possible agents who might be useful against the Islamic extremist target. Yet there will be enormous resistance inside the clandestine service to giving priority to the NOC corps in counterterrorism.

A similar push for more NOCs occurred in the early 1980s, when the Reaganites [conservative adherents of President Ronald Reagan], reacting to the ideologically driven force reductions of the '70s, decided to energize the CIA by expanding its clandestine capacity. The result: More NOCs were hired, but even more "inside" officers took to the field, including, for the first time, officially designated "counterterrorist" case officers. In the bigger stations and bases, case officers were stacked up like firewood. In many major cities, where fake business cover was easier to maintain, NOCs, too, started to pile up, and to search for something to justify their jobs. The number of mediocre "recruited" foreign agents exploded. The resignation rate among the more talented operatives rose rapidly.

Increasingly Irrelevant Agents

President Bush and Goss are well on the way to repeating the errors of Ronald Reagan and [former CIA director] William Casey. It should not require a detailed knowledge of agency history and operations for outsiders to see that most case officers, both "inside" officers and NOCs, have no relevance to the counterterrorist efforts.

The agency desperately needs to develop the culture and capacity to mimic the Islamic activist organizations that attract young male militants.

This is especially true for the operatives in the Near East division and the counterterrorism center, the two parts of the CIA most responsible for running operations against Islamic extremists. "Inside" officers simply cannot maneuver outside in an effective way. An officially covered case officer posted to Yemen trying to fish in fundamentalist circles would be immediately spotted by the internal security service, to say nothing of fundamentalists. And security concerns since Sept. 11 [2001] often seriously restrict the activities of CIA officers based in official U.S. facilities abroad.

Meanwhile, nonofficial cover officers working in the Middle East are, according to active-duty case officers, still mostly doing short-term work, flying in and out on brief assignments. Like their NOC colleagues elsewhere in the world, they are usually trapped by business cover that has little relevance to high-priority, dangerous targets.

Need for New Structure and Operatives

The agency desperately needs to develop the culture and capacity to mimic the Islamic activist organizations that attract young male militants. Creating such useful counterterrorist front organizations—Islamic charities and educational foundations—isn't labor-intensive, but it does take time. A dozen operatives, based at headquarters and as NOCs abroad, would be sufficient. But the clandestine service as currently structured and led would resist designing such a program, let alone trying to attract the people with the right backgrounds to accomplish the task. To go after the Islamic terrorist target in this way—to wean the CIA from its ever-growing dependence on Middle Eastern intelligence services and stations full of "inside" officers—would cause a revolt at Langley.

To my knowledge, there has never been a single study of the efficacy of CIA officers deployed against any target during the Cold War. The agency never once sat down and reviewed how and why case officers were stationed abroad. Certain targets would suddenly grow in importance—Cuba, Iran or Iraq—and large operational desks would become even larger task forces, all fueled by the assumption that bigger is better. According to active-duty officers, no serious evaluation has so far been done on the world of Islamic extremists, even though the number of officers assigned to this target has grown exponentially.

The CIA unquestionably needs to hire more operatives. It needs to have case officers better-schooled about the targets they chase. But unless the system is overhauled, the old blood will poison the new. In clandestine intelligence collection and covert action, bigger is rarely better. Only by thinking small, day after day, do case officers occasionally have the good fortune to make a contribution to their nation's defense.

10

The CIA Should Implement Modest Reforms, Not a Massive Overhaul

Bruce Berkowitz

Bruce Berkowitz is a research fellow at the Hoover Institution and a former CIA agent. He is also the author or coauthor of several books, including The New Face of War: How War Will Be Fought in the 21st Century *and* Best Truth: Intelligence in the Information Age.

Several commissions have investigated American intelligence failures, and most of the commissions have recommended similar reforms: creating "czars" who would take personal control of different aspects of the intelligence process, merging intelligence agencies or moving them around on the organizational chart, and giving additional authority to various agencies or persons. None of these reforms, however, would directly address the true problem facing the U.S. intelligence community: the fact that it lacks the capabilities necessary to create good intelligence on such emerging threats as terrorist groups and rogue states. Instead of undertaking the sorts of massive overhauls that the commissions have proposed, the Central Intelligence Agency (CIA) should instead focus on taking small steps that would enhance these specific capabilities.

U.S. intelligence agencies, already under fire for not anticipating the September 11 terrorist attacks, are now taking heat from a new crisis—the flap over Iraqi weapons of mass destruction (WMD). Intelligence organizations apparently overestimated Iraq's progress by a substantial margin. So far, no one has found significant stores of nuclear, biological, or chemical weapons in Iraq, and David Kay, who headed the team responsible for finding them, has said he does not believe further efforts are likely to change this result.

Proliferation of Commissions

President [George W.] Bush has appointed a commission to investigate the performance of U.S. intelligence on Iraq's WMD programs. This is good, because we need to establish an authoritative record of what happened so we are better prepared for the future.

But one has to wonder whether this commission—or any commission—can really fix the problems plaguing U.S. intelligence. During the past decade there have been several such commissions. Indeed, there has rarely been a moment when there was *not* a commission investigating U.S. intelligence. Consider the following:

- In 1994, Congress authorized the Commission on the Roles and Capabilities of the United States Intelligence Community to consider the future of U.S. intelligence following the Aldrich Ames espionage affair and the end of the Cold War [Ames is a former CIA agent who was arrested in 1994 and subsequently confessed to having been a Russian spy since 1985.] (This was the "Aspin-Brown Commission," named for former defense secretaries Les Aspin, who initially chaired it, and Harold Brown, who took over after Aspin died in May 1995.)

- In 1995, the House Permanent Select Committee on intelligence began its own study of the future of U.S. intelligence, as did organizations like the Council on Foreign Relations and the Twentieth Century Fund.

- In 1996, a commission headed by former director of Central Intelligence Robert Gates investigated alleged bias in a National Intelligence Estimate forecast of the North Korean ballistic missile threat.

- In 1998, a commission headed by retired admiral David Jeremiah investigated the failure of U.S. intelligence to anticipate India's nuclear test.

- In 2000, several boards and commissions investigated the failure of U.S. intelligence to provide warning of the attack by [terrorist group] Al Qaeda on the USS *Cole* in Yemen (to be sure, this was treated more as a security failure than an intelligence failure).

- Soon after President Bush took office, he approved National Security Policy Directive (NSPD) 5, which authorized a commission to perform a top-to-bottom assessment of U.S. intelligence capabilities and options for improving them.

- Shortly after the September 11, 2001, terrorist attacks, the House and Senate intelligence committees formed a joint inquiry to examine the performance of U.S. intelligence.

- In November 2002, the National Commission on Terrorist Attacks upon the United States—better known as the "9-11 Commission"—started its own investigation of the terrorist strike. Its report, which includes an examination of U.S. intelligence, is scheduled for completion later this year [2004].

Challenges for Commissions

With the most recent commission to investigate the Iraqi WMD flap, we have achieved a dubious milestone: We are now appointing new commissions to investigate U.S. intelligence faster than the existing ones can publish their findings.

This is even more remarkable when one considers how hard it is for any commission to have a significant effect on the intelligence process.

Commissions take months to convene, staff, and complete their work. Experience shows that commissions require, on average, a year or two to report their results—and even more time to declassify their reports so they can be released for public discussion. During this time, any passion officials might have had for fixing intelligence ebbs and the public's attention wanders to other matters.

Also, commissions have little clout. They are not connected to any of the real levers of power. They can't legislate, and they don't control the organizations they review. Because Congress is geared to the annual legislative calendar, it takes at least a year—or more—for it to act on a commission's recommendations and another year for the executive branch to implement the legislation. And, while all of this is going on, everyone is apt to put off major changes, saying that they should wait until any currently active commissions finish their work.

The problem is not that U.S. intelligence is poorly organized; the problem is that it lacks the specific capabilities it needs to deal with new threats such as terrorism rogue states, and proliferation of weapons of mass destruction.

Little wonder commissions often have the opposite of their intended effect—they stall reforms rather than facilitate them. To be fair, reforming U.S. intelligence is an inherently tough assignment. Like any bureaucracy, intelligence organizations are insulated from market forces, which compel businesses to adapt constantly to changing conditions, or elections, which reshape political bodies at regular intervals. But, unlike other bureaucracies, the intelligence community has features that make it especially resistant to change.

Most intelligence activities are classified, so data that experts in other fields take for granted—budgets, staffing, and performance—are unavailable and cannot be presented to the public to make a case for change. Imagine trying to analyze education policy without being able to discuss how many teachers are on the payrolls, how much the country spends on schooling, or how student test scores have varied over the past two decades, and you get an idea of the problem.

Reform: The Traditional Approach

Commissions have offered many, many recommendations for reforming U.S. intelligence, but most fit into three basic categories:

The first is creating czars. For example, the House-Senate joint inquiry into the September 11 [, 2001,] intelligence failure recommended creating a new Director of National Intelligence (DNI) who would be responsible for all intelligence resources other than those used by combat forces at the tactical level. The NSPD 5 study reportedly made a similar recommendation. The Aspin-Brown Commission proposed creating a new Deputy Director of Central Intelligence for Community Management in 1996, only to see the Senate Select Committee on Intelligence up the ante and propose creating three Assistant Directors of Central Intelligence (one for planning collection, one for planning analysis, and one for administration). As might be expected, the compromise was to adopt *both* proposals, so that by 1998 U.S. intelligence had four new executive positions.

The second is rearranging or restructuring organizations. Such reorganization was used in 1992, for example, when Air Force, CIA, and Navy satellite programs were integrated within the National Reconnaissance Office (NRO). It was also used when, in 1996, CIA and Defense Department imagery analysts were consolidated into the National Imagery and Mapping Agency (NIMA). More recently, according to press reports, the

NSPD 5 study recommended moving the National Security Agency (NSA), NRO, and NIMA out of the Defense Department and putting them under the direct control of the proposed DNI.

The third is giving officials or organizations new authorities. Logically enough, these proposals usually accompany the preceding two. For example, some experts who want to create a Director of National Intelligence propose giving that person authority to move people and money freely among intelligence agencies so that she or he can concentrate resources on the most important targets. Similarly, proposals for consolidating intelligence agencies are usually aimed at pulling authority for planning and coordination inside a single organization.

Creating czars, rearranging organizations, and assigning new authorities are all tempting, partly because they bring to mind the Goldwater-Nichols Act of 1986, which reformed the Defense Department. Most experts agree that Goldwater-Nichols improved U.S. military capabilities. They compare, for example, the failed Iranian hostage rescue operation in 1980 (when Army, Navy, and Air Force components did not cooperate effectively) with Operation Desert Storm in 1991 (when they did).

Reorganization Is Not the Answer

Alas, all these proposals may seem reasonable, but none of them address the most important problem facing U.S. intelligence. The problem is not that U.S. intelligence is poorly organized; the problem is that it lacks the specific capabilities it needs to deal with new threats such as terrorism rogue states, and proliferation of weapons of mass destruction. No amount of reorganization can compensate for that gap.

Also, reorganization is not the key to making intelligence organizations work together. The barriers that keep organizations from sharing information effectively and teaming up to crack hard targets could be solved with less drastic measures. For example, today organizations often impose their own rules for protecting information—despite repeated instructions to standardize them. As a result, organizational boundaries become information barriers. But this is a function of policy and the priority officials place on their agencies cooperating with each other, not how boxes are arranged on an organization chart.

That was the real reason the Goldwater-Nichols reforms were so effective. It wasn't just a matter of reorganization. Rather, Goldwater-Nichols forced the Army, Navy, and Air Force to concentrate on improving "jointness"—military jargon for the ability of services to work together. In practical terms, jointness meant the services had to design their communications and weapons systems to a common standard so they could communicate with one another, and officers were required to do a stint in an assignment outside their own service to broaden their perspectives.

Complex plans to reorganize big government organizations rarely turn out as planned and often have unintended consequences.

Proposals to yank intelligence organizations out of the Defense Department also overlook the role they play in combat operations today. The ability to feed electronic data to units on the battlefield through digital pipelines is essential for the kind of network-style warfare that has proved so effective in Iraq and Afghanistan. Combat forces use more of this data than anyone else. It seems odd that anyone would want to drag several intelligence organizations out of the Defense Department simply to create a new mega-organization whose main mission would be ... supporting the Defense Department.

True, we need digital intelligence for more than just military operations. But there are many ways to ensure other agencies can get these data—reserving a certain amount of priority use for non-defense agencies, giving them funds to collect the data themselves—or buying it from outside. Today, about the only digital information that government agencies have a unique advantage in collecting is communications intercepts.

Most of the rest—satellite imagery, for example—can be collected, processed, and analyzed in-house or bought commercially. Generally speaking, such competition among many sources improves the product.

Reform: An Alternate Approach

Intelligence reform ought to concentrate on creating new capabilities and removing obstacles that keep us from using our existing capabilities effectively.

Consider some of the specific problems U.S. intelligence currently faces:

- Because the CIA—the agency with the lead responsibility for espionage—relies so heavily on "official cover" (that is, disguising intelligence officers as run-of-the-mill U.S. officials), it has difficulty operating in countries where the United States has no representation. The use of official cover also limits opportunities to penetrate some of our most important targets, such as terrorist organizations or rogue states. . . .

- Security procedures, as noted previously, often prevent intelligence organizations from sharing data and working together effectively. Largely because of security, analysts are too insulated from both consumers and the targets they cover. Current security procedures make it hard for analysts, case officers, and technical specialists to cooperate in identifying and penetrating targets. It is often challenging for anyone inside the intelligence community to use outside information and expertise.

- The intelligence community as a whole does not have enough opportunities for the kind of entrepreneurship needed to develop out-of-the-box approaches to analysis, espionage, and technical collection. Because it is a mature organization, the intelligence community does not attract enough risk-takers. Those that do join are often frustrated by layers of bureaucracy and cumbersome procedures. As a result, U.S. intelligence is too slow to action new ideas or adopt new technologies and, with a few exceptions, it is hard for anyone to act outside established ways of doing business.

- Intelligence officials lack basic administrative tools that the private sector takes for granted—for example, software and accounting systems that tell managers how their analysts and collection assets are allocated at a given moment. As a results, they cannot reallocate people and resources effectively as requirements and conditions change—and the intelligence community as a whole lacks agility. . . .

The gathering consensus on the need for intelligence reform gives us a chance to address these problems—much as the consensus on the need for military reform transformed the Defense Department in the 1980s. But we need to be smart in how we do it. Remember that, in the real world, complex plans to reorganize big government organizations rarely turn out as planned and often have unintended consequences.

That's why I recommend focusing on two simple objectives: (1) removing barriers that keep all intelligence organizations from working together effectively and (2) beefing up the CIA so that it is better prepared for meeting the intelligence needs of nonmilitary users.

If we spent less effort debating organizational schemes, we might be able to focus the political will needed to make all intelligence organizations implement a truly common set of security standards that balance the importance of keeping secrets with the importance of sharing information. Then we could focus on strengthening the CIA, which has a unique role that no other agency can fill. Some of the steps that are urgently required include

- Creating a new, truly clandestine human intelligence service in the CIA to supplement the current Directorate of Operations. Its main mission would be penetrating foreign targets unilaterally, secretly, and without the assistance of other countries' intelligence services. It would be based outside CIA headquarters to ensure that it has effective cover. It would form relationships with American businesses and other organizations to establish presence in areas where the United States has no official representation. All members of this organization would be undercover throughout their careers and would be protected by the Intelligence Identities Act— meaning that disclosure of their connection to U.S. intelligence would be a crime.

- Refocusing the Directorate of Operations on the kinds of activities that it is most suited for: covert activities that do not require deep cover and which fully exploit the advantages of official cover. These include, for example, working with foreign intelligence agencies, recruiting "walk-ins" (foreigners from hostile regimes and organizations who volunteer their services to U.S. intelligence), organizing paramilitary operations like the ones that proved effective in Afghanistan, and providing covert security assistance to allies.

- Refocusing the Directorate of Science and Technology on the kinds of activities it has historically done well—

specifically, serving as a "skunk works" to field new technology fast in the classic style of, say, the U-2 reconnaissance aircraft or CORONA, the first imaging satellite.

- Making the Directorate of Intelligence the main window between the classified and unclassified worlds. Its analysts—who are not undercover and should not be encouraged to think they are undercover—should be given more opportunities, incentives, and funding to mix easily with people in academia, business, and the media and tap all publicly available sources of information and expertise.

In short, we would be much better off letting established organizations focus on their "core competencies"; make it easier for everyone to share information and work together; and create opportunities for new organizations to address new missions and attract risk-takers.

Reform via Executive Order

Most of these measures would not require major legislation. They could be accomplished by drafting a replacement for Executive Order [EO] 12333—the presidential directive that currently serves as the intelligence community's charter. EO 12333, which defines the roles, responsibilities, and prerogatives of intelligence organizations and the officials who run them, was signed by Ronald Reagan in 1982—more than 20 years ago. It was drafted when the Soviet Union was still an ominous threat, the Information Revolution was barely under way, and Osama bin Laden was just the obscure seventh son of a Yemeni construction tycoon.

A new executive order is needed that would be a faster, more effective vehicle for intelligence reform than a commission report or legislation. Such an order could also resolve the security barriers and other hurdles that currently keep intelligence agencies from working together more effectively. And, since it would have the authority of the president, it would have the required clout over department heads and other top officials down the line—especially if the president named a White House-level representative whose chief task would be to ensure it was implemented.

This isn't the time for grand designs. We need to focus on practical measures to develop real capabilities for dealing with the threats that face the country today.

11

The CIA Should Be Consolidated with Other U.S. Intelligence Agencies

National Commission on Terrorist Attacks Upon the United States

The National Commission on Terrorist Attacks Upon the United States, popularly known as the 9/11 Commission, was created by the federal government on November 27, 2002, to write the definitive account of the September 11, 2001, terrorist attacks and to make recommendations for preventing future attacks. The commission's members included former New Jersey governor Thomas H. Kean; former Indiana congressman Lee H. Hamilton; lawyers Richard Ben-Veniste and Fred F. Fielding; Jamie Gorelick, a former deputy attorney general of the United States; former Washington State senator Slade Gorton; Bob Kerrey, who was formerly governor of Nebraska and a United States senator; former secretary of the navy John F. Lehman; former Indiana congressman Timothy J. Roemer; and former Illinois governor James Thompson. The commission submitted its report on July 22, 2004, and disbanded one month later.

The U.S. intelligence community is not sufficiently organized to deal with the threat of terrorism against the United States. The fifteen separate agencies that make up the intelligence community are each focused on their own separate areas of responsibility and are poorly coordinated, making it difficult for them to create a "big picture" view of the terrorist threat. To solve this problem, the intelligence community should be restructured so

National Commission on Terrorist Attacks Upon the United States, excerpt from *9/11 Commission Report*. Washington, DC: Government Printing Office, 2004.

that it is more unified. All of the U.S. intelligence agencies should answer to a single national intelligence director, and a single national counterterrorism center should be created.

As presently configured, the national security institutions of the U.S. government are still the institutions constructed to win the Cold War. The United States confronts a very different world today. Instead of facing a few very dangerous adversaries, the United States confronts a number of less visible challenges that surpass the boundaries of traditional nation-states and call for quick, imaginative, and agile responses.

The men and women of the World War II generation rose to the challenges of the 1940s and 1950s. They restructured the government so that it could protect the country. That is now the job of the generation that experienced 9/11. Those attacks showed, emphatically, that ways of doing business rooted in a different era are just not good enough. Americans should not settle for incremental ad hoc adjustments to a system designed generations ago for a world that no longer exists.

We recommend significant changes in the organization of the government. We know that the quality of the people is more important than the quality of the wiring diagrams. Some of the saddest aspects of the 9/11 story are the outstanding efforts of so many individual officials straining, often without success, against the boundaries of the possible. Good people can overcome bad structures. They should not have to.

The United States has the resources and the people. The government should combine them more effectively, achieving unity of effort. We offer five major recommendations to do that:

- unifying strategic intelligence and operational planning against Islamist terrorists across the foreign-domestic divide with a National Counterterrorism Center;

- unifying the intelligence community with a new National Intelligence Director;

- unifying the many participants in the counterterrorism effort and their knowledge in a network-based information-sharing system that transcends traditional governmental boundaries;

- unifying and strengthening congressional oversight to improve quality and accountability; and

- strengthening the FBI [Federal Bureau of Investigation] and homeland defenders.

Joint Action

Much of the public commentary about the 9/11 attacks has dealt with "lost opportunities".... These are often characterized as problems of "watchlisting," of "information sharing" or of "connecting the dots."... These labels are too narrow. They describe the symptoms, not the disease.

The effort of fighting terrorism has flooded over many of the usual agency boundaries because of its sheer quality and energy.

In [the events investigated by the commission], no one was firmly in charge of managing the case and able to draw relevant intelligence from anywhere in the government, assign responsibilities across the agencies (foreign or domestic), track progress, and quickly bring obstacles up to the level where they could be resolved. Responsibility and accountability were diffuse.

The agencies cooperated, some of the time. But even such cooperation as there was is not the same thing as joint action. When agencies cooperate, one defines the problem and seeks help with it. When they act jointly, the problem and options for action are defined differently from the start. Individuals from different backgrounds come together in analyzing a case and planning how to manage it.

In our hearings we regularly asked witnesses: Who is the quarterback? The other players are in their positions, doing their jobs. But who is calling the play that assigns roles to help them execute as a team?

Since 9/11, those issues have not been resolved. In some ways joint work has gotten better, and in some ways worse. The effort of fighting terrorism has flooded over many of the usual agency boundaries because of its sheer quantity and energy. Attitudes have changed. Officials are keenly conscious of trying to avoid the mistakes of 9/11. They try to share information. They circulate—even to the President—practically every reported threat, however dubious.

Partly because of all this effort, the challenge of coordinating it has multiplied. Before 9/11, the CIA [Central Intelligence Agency] was plainly the lead agency confronting al Qaeda. The FBI played a very secondary role. The engagement of the departments of Defense and State was more episodic.

- Today the CIA is still central. But the FBI is much more active, along with other parts of the Justice Department.

- The Defense Department effort is now enormous. Three of its unified commands, each headed by a four-star general, have counterterrorism as a primary mission: Special Operations Command, Central Command (both headquartered in Florida), and Northern Command (headquartered in Colorado).

- A new Department of Homeland Security combines formidable resources in border and transportation security, along with analysis of domestic vulnerability and other tasks.

- The State Department has the lead on many . . . foreign policy tasks. . . .

- At the White House, the National Security Council (NSC) now is joined by a parallel presidential advisory structure, the Homeland Security Council.

So far we have mentioned two reasons for joint action—the virtue of joint planning and the advantage of having someone in charge to ensure a unified effort. There is a third: the simple shortage of experts with sufficient skills. The limited pool of critical experts—for example, skilled counterterrorism analysts and linguists—is being depleted. Expanding these capabilities will require not just money, but time.

Primary responsibility for terrorism analysis has been assigned to the Terrorist Threat Integration Center (TTIC), created in 2003, based at the CIA headquarters but staffed with representatives of many agencies, reporting directly to the Director of Central Intelligence [DCI]. Yet the CIA houses another intelligence "fusion" center: the Counterterrorist Center that played such a key role before 9/11. A third major analytic unit is at Defense, in the Defense Intelligence Agency [DIA]. A fourth, concentrating more on homeland vulnerabilities, is at the Department of Homeland Security. The FBI is in the process of building the analytic capability it has long lacked, and it also has the Terrorist Screening Center.

The U.S. government cannot afford so much duplication of effort. There are not enough experienced experts to go around. The duplication also places extra demands on already hard-pressed single-source national technical intelligence collectors like the National Security Agency.

Combining Joint Intelligence and Joint Action

A smart government would *integrate* all sources of information to see the enemy as a whole. Integrated all-source analysis should also inform and shape strategies to collect more intelligence. Yet the Terrorist Threat Integration Center, while it has primary responsibility for terrorism analysis, is formally proscribed from having any oversight or operational authority and is not part of any operational entity, other than reporting to the director of central intelligence. . . .

The problem is nearly intractable because of the way the government is currently structured. Lines of operational authority run to the expanding executive departments, and they are guarded for understandable reasons: the DCI commands the CIA's personnel overseas; the secretary of defense will not yield to others in conveying commands to military forces; the Justice Department will not give up the responsibility of deciding whether to seek arrest warrants. But the result is that each agency or department needs its own intelligence apparatus to support the performance of its duties. It is hard to "break down stovepipes" when there are so many stoves that are legally and politically entitled to have cast-iron pipes of their own.

A common set of personnel standards for intelligence can create a group of professionals better able to operate in joint activities.

Recalling the Goldwater-Nichols legislation of 1986 [which centralized the commands of the Army, Navy, Air Force and Marines], Secretary [of Defense Donald] Rumsfeld reminded us that to achieve better joint capability, each of the armed services had to "give up some of their turf and authorities and prerogatives." Today, he said, the executive branch is "stovepiped much like the four services were nearly 20 years ago." He wondered if it might be appropriate to ask agencies to "give up some of their existing turf and authority in exchange for a stronger, faster, more efficient government wide joint effort." Privately, other key officials have made the same point to us.

We therefore propose a new institution: a civilian-led unified joint command for counterterrorism. It should combine strategic intelligence and joint operational planning.

In the Pentagon's Joint Staff, which serves the chairman of the Joint Chiefs of Staff, intelligence is handled by the J-2 directorate, operational planning by J-3, and overall policy by J-5. Our concept combines the J-2 and J-3 functions (intelligence and operational planning) in one agency, keeping overall policy coordination where it belongs, in the National Security Council.

Recommendation: We recommend the establishment of a National Counterterrorism Center (NCTC), built on the foundation of the existing Terrorist Threat Integration Center (TTIC). Breaking the older mold of national government organization, this NCTC should be a center for joint operational planning *and* joint intelligence, staffed by personnel from the various agencies. The head of the NCTC should have authority to evaluate the performance of the people assigned to the Center.

- Such a joint center should be developed in the same spirit that guided the military's creation of unified joint commands, or the shaping of earlier national agencies like the National Reconnaissance Office, which was formed to organize the work of the CIA and several defense agencies in space.

NCTC—Intelligence. The NCTC should lead strategic analysis, pooling all-source intelligence, foreign and domestic, about transnational terrorist organizations with global reach. It should develop *net* assessments (comparing enemy capabilities and intentions against U.S. defenses and countermeasures). It should also provide warning. It should do this work by drawing on the efforts of the CIA, FBI, Homeland Security, and other departments and agencies. It should task collection requirements both inside and outside the United States.

- The intelligence function (J-2) should build on the existing TTIC structure and remain distinct, as a national intelligence center, within the NCTC. As the government's principal knowledge bank on Islamist terrorism, with the main responsibility for strategic analysis and net assessment, it should absorb a significant portion of the analytical talent now residing in the CIA's Counterterrorist Center and the DIA's Joint Intelligence Task Force—Combatting Terrorism (JITF-CT).

NCTC—Operations. The NCTC should perform joint planning. The plans would assign operational responsibilities to lead agencies, such as State, the CIA, the FBI, Defense and its combatant commands, Homeland Security, and other agencies. The NCTC should *not* direct the actual execution of these operations, leaving that job to the agencies. The NCTC would then track implementation; it would look across the foreign-domestic divide and across agency boundaries, updating plans to follow through on cases.

- The joint operational planning function (J-3) will be new to the TTIC structure. The NCTC can draw on analogous work now being done in the CIA and every other involved department of the government, as well as reaching out to knowledgeable officials in state and local agencies throughout the United States.

- The NCTC should *not* be a policymaking body. Its operations and planning should follow the policy direction of the president and the National Security Council.

NCTC—Authorities. The head of the NCTC should be appointed by the president, and should be equivalent in rank to a deputy head of a cabinet department. The head of the NCTC would report to the national intelligence director, placed in the Executive Office of the President. The head of the NCTC would thus also report indirectly to the president. This official's nomination should be confirmed by the Senate and he or she should testify to the Congress, as is the case now with other statutory presidential offices, like the U.S. trade representative.

- To avoid the fate of other entities with great nominal authority and little real power, the head of the NCTC must have the right to concur in the choices of personnel to lead the operating entities of the departments and agencies focused on counterterrorism, specifically including the head of the Counterterrorist Center, the head of the FBI's Counterterrorism Division, the commanders of the Defense Department's Special Operations Command and Northern Command, and the State Deparunent's coordinator for counterterrorism. The head of the NCTC should also work with the director of the Office of Management and Budget in developing the president's counterterrorism budget. . . .

The Need for a Change

The need to restructure the intelligence community grows out of six problems that have become apparent before and after 9/11:

- *Structural barriers to performing joint intelligence work.* National intelligence is still organized around the collection disciplines of the home agencies, not the joint mission. The importance of integrated, all-source analysis cannot be overstated. Without it, it is not possible to "connect the dots." No one component holds all the relevant information.

By contrast, in organizing national defense, the Goldwater-Nichols legislation of 1986 created joint commands for operations in the field, the Unified Command Plan. The services—the Army, Navy, Air Force, and Marine Corps—organize, train, and equip their people and units to perform their missions. Then they assign personnel and units to the joint combatant commander, like the commanding general of the Central Command (CENTCOM). The Goldwater-Nichols Act required officers to serve tours outside their service in order to win promotion. The culture of the Defense Department was transformed, its collective mind-set moved from service-specific to "joint;" and its operations became more integrated.

- *Lack of common, standards and practices across the foreign-domestic divide.* The leadership of the intelligence community should be able to pool information gathered overseas with information gathered in the United States, holding the work—wherever it is done—to a common standard of quality in how it is collected, processed (e.g., translated), reported, shared, and analyzed. A common set of personnel standards for intelligence can create a group of professionals better able to operate in joint activities, transcending their own service-specific mind-sets.

- *Divided management of national intelligence capabilities.* While the CIA was once "central" to our national intelligence capabilities, following the end of the Cold War it has been less able to influence the use of the nation's imagery and signals intelligence capabilities in three national agencies housed within the Department of Defense: the National Security Agency, the National Geospatial-Intelligence Agency, and the National Reconnaissance Office. One of the lessons learned from the 1991 Gulf War was the value of national intelligence systems (satellites in particular) in precision warfare. Since that war, the department has appropriately drawn these agencies into its transformation of the military. Helping to orchestrate this transformation is the under secretary of defense for intelligence, a position established by Congress after 9/11. An unintended consequence of these developments has been the far greater demand made by Defense on technical systems, leaving the DCI less able to influence how these technical resources are allocated and used.

- *Weak capacity to set priorities and move resources.* The agencies are mainly organized around what they collect or the way they collect it. But the priorities for collection are national. As the DCI makes hard choices about moving resources, he or she must have the power to reach across agencies and reallocate effort.

- *Too many jobs.* The DCI now has at least three jobs. He is expected to run a particular agency, the CIA. He is expected to manage the loose confederation of agencies that is the intelligence community. He is expected to be the analyst in chief for the government, sifting evidence and directly briefing the President as his principal intelligence adviser. No recent DCI has been able to do all three effectively. Usually what loses out is management of the intelligence community, a difficult task even in the best case because the DCI's current authorities are weak. With so much to do, the DCI often has not used even the authority he has. . . .

- *Too complex and secret.* Over the decades, the agencies and the rules surrounding the intelligence community have accumulated to a depth that practically defies public comprehension. There are now 15 agencies or parts of agencies in the intelligence community. The community and the DCI's authorities have become arcane matters, understood only by initiates after long study. Even the most basic information about how much money is actually allocated to or within the intelligence community and most of its key components is shrouded from public view.

National Intelligence Director

Recommendation: The current position of Director of Central Intelligence should be replaced by a National Intelligence Director with two main areas of responsibility: (1) to

oversee national intelligence centers on specific subjects of interest across the U.S. government and (2) to manage the national intelligence program and oversee the agencies that contribute to it.

First, the National Intelligence Director should oversee *national intelligence centers* to provide all-source analysis and plan intelligence operations for the whole government on major problems.

- One such problem is counterterrorism. In this case, we believe that the center should be the intelligence entity (formerly TTIC) inside the National Counterterrorism Center we have proposed. It would sit there alongside the operations management unit we described earlier, with both making up the NCTC, in the Executive Office of the President. Other national intelligence centers—for instance, on counterproliferation, crime and narcotics, and China—would be housed in whatever department or agency is best suited for them.

- The National Intelligence Director would retain the present DCI's role as the principal intelligence adviser to the president. We hope the president will come to look directly to the directors of the national intelligence centers to provide all-source analysis in their areas of responsibility, balancing the advice of these intelligence chiefs against the contrasting viewpoints that may be offered by department heads at State, Defense, Homeland Security, Justice, and other agencies.

Second, the National Intelligence Director should manage the national intelligence program and oversee the component agencies of the intelligence community. . . .

- The National Intelligence Director would manage this national effort with the help of three deputies, each of whom would also hold a key position in one of the component agencies.

- foreign intelligence (the head of the CIA)

- defense intelligence (the under secretary of defense for intelligence)

- homeland intelligence (the FBI's executive assistant director for intelligence or the under secretary of homeland security for information analysis and infrastructure protection)

Other agencies in the intelligence community would coordinate their work within each of these three areas, largely staying housed in the same departments or agencies that support them now.

Returning to the analogy of the Defense Department's organization, these three deputies—like the leaders of the Army, Navy, Air Force, or Marines—would have the job of acquiring the systems, training the people, and executing the operations planned by the national intelligence centers.

And, just as the combatant commanders also report to the secretary of defense, the directors of the national intelligence centers—e.g., for counterproliferation, crime and narcotics, and the rest—also would report to the National Intelligence Director. . . .

- The National Intelligence Director would set personnel policies to establish standards for education and training and facilitate assignments at the national intelligence centers and across agency lines. The National Intelligence Director also would set information sharing and information technology policies to maximize data sharing, as well as policies to protect the security of information. . . .

- Too many agencies now have an opportunity to say no to change. The National Intelligence Director should participate in an NSC executive committee that can resolve differences in priorities among the agencies and bring the major disputes to the president for decision. . . .

We are wary of too easily equating government management problems with those of the private sector. But we have noticed that some very large private firms rely on a powerful CEO [chief executive officer] who has significant control over how money is spent and can hire or fire leaders of the major divisions, assisted by a relatively modest staff, while leaving responsibility for execution in the operating divisions.

The Role of the CIA

There are disadvantages to separating the position of National Intelligence Director from the job of heading the CIA. For example, the National Intelligence Director will not head a major agency of his or her own and may have a weaker base of support. But we believe that these disadvantages are outweighed by several other considerations:

- The National Intelligence Director must be able to directly oversee intelligence collection inside the United States. Yet law and custom has counseled against giving such a plain domestic role to the head of the CIA.

- The CIA will be one among several claimants for funds in setting national priorities. The National Intelligence Director should not be both one of the advocates and the judge of them all.

- Covert operations tend to be highly tactical, requiring close attention. The National Intelligence Director should rely on the relevant joint mission center to oversee these details, helping to coordinate closely with the White House. The CIA will be able to concentrate on building the capabilities to carry out such operations and on providing the personnel who will be directing and executing such operations in the field.

- Rebuilding the analytic and human intelligence collection capabilities of the CIA should be a full-time effort, and the director of the CIA should focus on extending its comparative advantages.

Recommendation: The CIA Director should emphasize (a) rebuilding the CIA's analytic capabilities; (b) transforming the clandestine service by building its human intelligence capabilities; (c) developing a stronger language program, with high standards and sufficient financial incentives; (d) renewing emphasis on recruiting diversity among operations officers so they can blend more easily in foreign cities; (e) ensuring a seamless relationship between human source collection and signals collection at the operational level; and (f) stressing a better balance between unilateral and liaison operations.

The United States cannot afford to build two separate capabilities for carrying out secret military operations . . . and secretly training foreign military or paramilitary forces.

The CIA should retain responsibility for the direction and execution of clandestine and covert operations, as assigned by the relevant national intelligence center and authorized by the National Intelligence Director and the president. This would include propaganda, renditions, and nonmilitary disruption. We believe, however, that one important area of responsibility should change.

Recommendation: Lead responsibility for directing and executing paramilitary operations, whether clandestine or covert, should shift to the Defense Department. There it should be consolidated with the capabilities for training, direction, and execution of such operations already being developed in the Special Operations Command.

- Before 9/11, the CIA did not invest in developing a robust capability to conduct paramilitary operations with U.S. personnel. It relied on proxies instead, organized by CIA operatives without the requisite military training. The results were unsatisfactory.

- Whether the price is measured in either money or people, the United States cannot afford to build two separate capabilities for carrying out secret military operations, secretly operating standoff missiles, and secretly training foreign military or paramilitary forces. The United States should concentrate responsibility and necessary legal authorities in one entity.

- The post-9/11 Afghanistan precedent of using joint CIA-military teams for covert and clandestine operations was a good one. We believe this proposal to be consistent with it. Each agency would concentrate on its comparative advantages in building capabilities for joint missions. The operation itself would be planned in common.

- The CIA has a reputation for agility in operations. The military has a reputation for being methodical and cumbersome. We do not know if these stereotypes match current reality; they may also be one more symptom of the civil-military misunderstandings. . . . It is a problem to be resolved in policy guidance and agency management, not in the creation of redundant, overlapping capabilities and authorities in such sensitive work. The CIA's experts should be integrated into the military's training, exercises, and planning. To quote a CIA official now serving in the field: "One fight, one team."

12

The CIA Should Remain an Independent Agency

Richard A. Posner

Richard A. Posner is a senior lecturer at the University of Chicago Law School and was formerly chief judge of the U.S. Court of Appeals for the Seventh Circuit. He is the author of several books, including Preventing Surprise Attacks: Intelligence Reform in the Wake of 9/11, *from which the following selection is excerpted.*

Centralizing all of the U.S. intelligence agencies under the control of one person or entity is not the best way to fix the intelligence failures that led to the September 11, 2001, terrorist attacks. Divisions within a centralized agency are just as prone to withholding information, launching turf wars, and otherwise failing to cooperate as completely separate agencies are. In addition, consolidating intelligence agencies would result in a lack of diversity and a higher tendency toward groupthink. It is important to have multiple intelligence agencies researching problems from different angles and competing to find the best solutions.

Coordination of intelligence agencies is an imperative; centralization may not be. Before the Intelligence Reform Act, the agencies were coordinated in a variety of ways (most of which will continue): through committees in the executive branch, such as the National Security Council and, though much less important, the President's Foreign Intelligence Advisory Board and Intelligence Oversight Board; through the Office of Management and Budget, which coordinates the budget proposals of the different departments and agencies in the executive branch; through a variety of ad hoc task forces and informal contacts; through congressional committees; by the CIA [Central Intelligence Agency] director in his capacity as Director of Central Intelligence and thus the chairman of the board of the intelligence community; within the CIA through fusion centers, such as the Counterintelligence Center; and through fusion centers outside the CIA, such as the National Intelligence Council and the new National Counterterrorism Center, which supersedes the CIA's Terrorist Threat Integration Center. So loose a system of coordination was bound to produce gaps and overlaps, but the latter, at least, are not necessarily a bad thing to have. Redundancy is a standard method of increasing safety, and safety is the business of intelligence. . . .

Intelligence Sharing

The 9/11 Commission blamed the failure to anticipate the 9/11 attacks mainly on inadequate sharing of intelligence among the different intelligence agencies and thought a more centralized intelligence structure an indispensable part of the cure. The cure may not fit the disease. The different intelligence agencies are not actually being merged, and anyway information sometimes flows more freely between organizations than within them. The problem of sharing intelligence information is almost as acute within agencies like the CIA (recall the reluctance of the operations branch to share information with the analytic branch), and especially the FBI [Federal Bureau of Investigation], as between agencies—and in the case of the FBI, maybe more so. An agency's sense of common mission can be occluded by internal tensions. The criminal investigators in the FBI may feel more threatened by the Bureau's intelligence officers than by the Border Patrol in the Department of Homeland Security and may be more willing to cooperate with local police, who are engaged in the same kind of work as they, than with the Bureau's own intelligence officers. Competition for budget may be more intense within than across agencies, and likewise jockeying for the attention and support of superiors.

The [intelligence] system is likely to be more productive to the extent that it consists of diverse and not merely multiple producers.

Any benefits in the way of better sharing of intelligence among intelligence agencies as a result of greater centralization are likely, moreover, to be purchased at the cost of increased uniformity in personnel policies, intelligence methods, and organizational traditions and cultures. Those cultures can differ markedly; the State Department, the culture of which could not be more different from that of the CIA, has its own intelligence agency, the Bureau of Intelligence and Research. Although I am calling uniformity a "cost," it might seem a very good thing simply on grounds of economy. But differences among agencies in practices, recruitment, traditions, and other characteristics that give an organization a unique perspective promote not only competitive energy and team spirit but also diversity of approach, perspective, and outlook. Maybe diverse agencies don't share information as well as agencies do that are as like one another as peas in a pod (though this is uncertain), but maybe they produce more and better information, and the benefit may exceed the cost.

Diversity of Opinions

How might diversity promote the production of information? Consider innovation in the private sector, now widely understood as a quasi-Darwinian process: one almost of trial and error, in which the market selects from among diverse approaches whose relative promise cannot be assessed in advance, much as nature selects from among variant competing life-forms—the products of random mutation—those best adapted to their environment. The greater the diversity of life-forms to choose from, the more rapid and complete the adaptation to the environment, corresponding in human society to maximizing welfare through technological progress. Completing the analogy, a multiplicity of independent sources of inventive activity may be superior to a centralized process. Consider "high-flex" Silicon Valley firms, with their "change culture" upon which there is great consensus. They will have shallow hierarchies and significant local autonomy. Such firms will resist the hierarchical accouterments of seniority and rank—and they will resist functional specialization which restricts the flow of ideas and destroys the sense of commonality of purpose," [writes David J. Teece.]

Another word for innovation is information, which is a synonym for intelligence—so the business of an intelligence system is innovation; and the system is likely to be more productive to the extent that it consists of diverse and not merely multiple producers: Remember that perception is a selection, from the mass of sense data, that is guided by preconception. A diversity of preconceptions will generate a richer selection of relevant information to analyze and a broader range of perspectives among the analysts. We want analysts to be sampling from the broadest possible range of data and to be drawing inferences from their samples with different mind-sets. Differently acculturated intelligence officers will notice different things. So here is a potential benefit of limiting sharing of information among intelligence officers: to avoid premature consensus. It is also an argument for encouraging some mid-career lateral entry into the CIA.

Another name for preconception, one that ties intelligence more directly to innovation, is theory. We make sense of the world by formulating theories to explain and predict phenomena. The theories are influenced by facts, but once formulated they become lenses through which to view and interpret new facts. If the theories are wrong, the interpretations they impose will impede the process by which theories are overthrown by confrontation with inconvenient facts. Whether the theory is that the Japanese threat to Pearl Harbor is sabotage or that al Qaeda will only attack the U.S. overseas, the falsity of the theory is the critical obstacle to anticipating the attack, because the theory obscures, dissolves, and distorts facts that would otherwise raise a warning flag. So we want an intelligence culture in which the regnant theories are constantly being challenged, not by devil's advocates, who are merely stage challengers, but by people who really see the world differently; and for those people to have a voice and be heard—for a genuine clash of theories to occur, as in science—requires a diverse intelligence system, implying a flat structure with loose rather than tight control over its component parts.

Bureaucracy and Uniformity

Diversity is difficult to achieve within a single agency because . . . effective control of an organization requires imposing a high degree of uniformity on the employees. Large organizations are bureaucracies governed by rules that can furnish clear guidance only by abstracting from many of the different ways in which particular tasks might be performed and particular employees compensated, motivated, supervised, and so on, and establishing uniform pay scales, working conditions, retirement programs, promotion criteria. The need for uniformity is another way of explaining why heterogeneity limits the expansion of organizations. In principle, a single organization could be loose knit, permitting a thousand flowers to bloom within it—more like a confederation, an alliance, than like an organization. But in practice, at least in large organizations, the centrifugal forces would be too great; some minimum homogeneity is necessary if management is to maintain control.

The 9/11 Commission did not propose fusing all our intelligence services into a single agency. But the CEO [chief executive officer]-like role that it envisaged for the Director of National Intelligence conceived of the different services as being like the divisions of a single business firm. How far unification will proceed under the Intelligence Reform Act is, at this writing, unclear. But maybe too far. For although it isn't possible to model the U.S. intelligence system on a "high-flex" Silicon Valley firm, the system could be gravely weakened by being moved too far in the opposite direction, toward the tight bureaucracy symbolized by the U.S. Postal Service.

13

The CIA Should Be Abolished

Chalmers Johnson

Chalmers Johnson is a professor emeritus of Asian studies and political science at the University of California. He is the author of several books, including Blowback: The Costs and Consequences of American Empire *and* The Sorrows of Empire: Militarism, Secrecy, and the End of the Republic.

The Central Intelligence Agency (CIA) is a failure and a danger to the United States. Its attempted coups against foreign governments have led to retaliatory terrorist attacks against the United States, and its intelligence estimates are consistently worse than those provided by researchers who work with nonclassified sources. In addition, its secrecy makes it difficult to hold the agency accountable for its failures. The CIA and other secret agencies should be abolished, and the government should instead use a transparent, public process to make intelligence estimates.

Adm. Stansfield Turner, former director of central intelligence from 1977 to 1981, recommended in a *New York Times* op-ed earlier this month [February 2004] that U.S. intelligence operations could be improved by adding another layer of bureaucracy to what he admits is a flawed system of overlapping spy agencies, interagency rivalries and vested interests.

I have a better idea: Why don't we abolish the CIA and make public, as the Constitution requires, the billions spent

Chalmers Johnson, "Improve the CIA? Better to Abolish It," *San Francisco Chronicle*, February 22, 2004. Copyright © 2004 San Francisco Chronicle. Reproduced by permission of the author.

by the intelligence agencies under the control of the Department of Defense so that Congress might have a fighting chance in doing oversight?

Catastrophically Wrong Intelligence

A few years ago, the late Sen. Daniel Patrick Moynihan, D-N.Y., suggested that we dismantle the agency that has so often produced catastrophically wrong national intelligence estimates. He was outraged by CIA calculations throughout the [Ronald] Reagan and elder [George] Bush years that overstated the size of the Soviet economy by 50 percent and led our government into a weapons-spending spree that left us the world's largest debtor nation. According to President George W. Bush and his chief weapons inspector, David Kay, the agency has done it again, misleading the nation about the alleged menace posed by the ousted president of Iraq, Saddam Hussein.

Our Intelligence apparatus has been flawed from the day it was created. Allegedly intended to prevent a surprise attack on our country comparable to the Dec. 7, 1941, Japanese assault on Pearl Harbor, the agency was supposed to be a central clearinghouse for intelligence collected by many different bodies throughout the government—including the military services, the signals intercepts of the National Security Agency, counterespionage by the FBI [Federal Bureau of Investigation], as well as its own efforts to recruit and run foreign agents.

The President's Secret Army

But in fact, intelligence collecting and analysis would quickly become camouflage for a private secret army at the personal command of the president devoted to dirty tricks, covert overthrows of foreign governments and planting disinformation—as well as efforts to counter similar operations by the Soviet Union.

According to an internal CIA history, the éminence grise of secret operations in the United States and founder of the

CIA's predecessor, the Office of Strategic Services during World War II, Maj. Gen. William J. "Wild Bill" Donovan "saw intelligence analysis as a convenient cover for subversive operations abroad." From our first covert overthrow of a foreign government, the ouster of the prime minister of Iran in 1953 in order to install the young shah Reza Pahlavi, the path to fame and success within the agency was in secret operations, not in writing intelligence estimates. That is certainly the pecking order I observed when I served as an outside consultant to the Office of National Estimates of the CIA from 1967 to 1973.

The high-security classifications of national intelligence estimates are not there to protect sources ... but to hide the incompetence and lack of serious effort that goes into producing them.

Since the overthrow of the Iranian government in 1953, the CIA has engaged in similar disguised assaults on the governments of Guatemala (1954); the Congo (1960); Cuba (1961); Brazil (1964); Indonesia (1965); Vietnam, Laos and Cambodia (1961–73); Greece (1967); Chile (1973); Afghanistan (1979 to the present); El Salvador, Guatemala and Nicaragua (1980s); and Iraq (1991 to the present)—to name only the most obvious cases. These operations have generated numerous terrorist attacks and other forms of retaliation—what the CIA calls "blowback"—against the United States by peoples on the receiving end. Because covert operations are secret from the people of the United States (if not their targets), when retaliation hits, as it did so spectacularly on Sept. 11, 2001, Americans do not have the information to put it into context or understand it.

Superior Public Intelligence

As for the CIA's prewar intelligence on Iraq, the recently appointed commission of prestigious Americans to investigate its shortcomings is unlikely to be able to tell us anything we do not already know. Much of what now is clearly true could have been discovered by talking to experts perfectly willing to be on the public record or simply researched on the Internet. Sam Gardiner, a retired Air Force colonel who taught for years at the National War College and who compiled a "net assessment" of how Iraq would look after a successful U.S. attack, predicted with devastating accuracy the chaos that ensued and did so on the basis of information freely available.

Who needs a CIA that so regularly underperforms in comparison to what is available on the open market? The high-security classifications of national intelligence estimates are not there to protect sources (no sources are ever mentioned in them), but to hide the incompetence and lack of serious effort that goes into producing them.

If Bush had appointed an investigative commission headed by Valerie Plame (the outed CIA wife of Ambassador Joseph Wilson) and composed of such journalists as Seymour Hersh, Jim Follows, Stephen Kinzer and Paul Krugman, its report would probably be worth reading. Short of that, I propose abolishing the agency and reducing our annual deficit by about $30 billion.

Organizations to Contact

American Enterprise Institute for Public Policy Research (AEI)
1150 17th St. NW, Washington, DC   20036
(202) 862-5800 • fax: (202) 862-7177
Web site: www.aei.org

AEI is a conservative think tank that studies both foreign and domestic policy. It maintains an extensive archive of short publications relating to international affairs and defense issues on its Web site. AEI's print publications include the bimonthly magazine the *American Enterprise* and numerous books.

Brookings Institution
1775 Massachusetts Ave., NW, Washington, DC   20036-2188
(202) 797-6000 • fax: (202) 797-6004
e-mail: brookinfo@brookings.edu
Web site: www.brookings.edu

Founded in 1927, the institution is a liberal research and education organization that publishes material on economics, government, and foreign policy. It strives to serve as a bridge between scholarship and public policy, bringing new knowledge to the attention of decision makers and providing scholars with improved insight into public policy issues. Its publications include the quarterly *Brookings Review*, the "Policy Briefs" series of papers, and books, including *State of the Struggle: Report on the Battle Against Global Terrorism*.

Center for American Progress
1333 H St. NW, 10th Floor, Washington, DC   20005
(202) 682-1611
e-mail: progress@americanprogress.org
Web site: www.americanprogress.org

The Center for American Progress is a progressive think tank dedicated to improving the lives of Americans through ideas and action. National security, including intelligence, is one of the center's major research areas. It makes a variety of op-eds and other papers available for free on its Web site.

Center for International Policy (CIP)
1717 Massachusetts Ave. NW, Suite 801
Washington, DC   20036
(202) 232-3317 • fax: (202) 232-3440
e-mail: cip@ciponline.org
Web site: www.ciponline.org

CIP works to promote a U.S. foreign policy based on cooperation, demilitarization, and respect for human rights. CIP's National Security Program opposes the militarization and centralization of the U.S. intelligence community and supports stronger Congressional oversight of intelligence. CIP publishes a series of International Policy Reports about intelligence and other issues; titles in the series include *Blueprint for Intelligence Reform* and *National Intelligence: The Dereliction of Congressional Oversight.*

Central Intelligence Agency (CIA)
Office of Public Affairs, Washington, DC   20505
(703) 482-0623 • fax: (703) 482-1739
Web site: www.cia.gov

The CIA is a government agency that is responsible for collecting and analyzing intelligence about foreign affairs and transmitting that intelligence to policy makers. The CIA makes a variety of unclassified materials available for free on its Web site, including *The World Fact Book* and the journal *Studies in Intelligence.*

The Century Foundation
41 E. 70th St., New York, NY   10021
(212) 535-4441 • fax: (212) 535-7534
e-mail: info@tcf.org

The CIA

Web site: www.tcf.org

This left-leaning research foundation, formerly known as the Twentieth Century Fund, sponsors analysis of many issues, including American foreign policy. It also sponsors the Homeland Security Project, which has intelligence reform as one of its major issues. The Century Foundation publishes numerous books and papers, including *Assessing the 9/11 Panel's Recommendations for Reshaping American Intelligence.*

Council on Foreign Relations (CFR)
58 E. 68th St., New York, NY   10021
(212) 434-9400 • fax: (212) 434-9800
Web site: www.cfr.og

CFR is a nonpartisan resource for information on and analysis of international and national security—issues. It operates a think tank that conducts research on foreign affairs, holds debates that include government officials and other global leaders, and sponsors task forces that produce reports on a variety of international issues. Articles, reports, and op-ed pieces by CFR members are available on its Web site, and it publishes the journal *Foreign Affairs.*

Federation of American Scientists (FAS)
1717 K St. NW Suite 209, Washington, DC   20036
(202) 546-3300 • fax: (202) 675-1010
Web site: www.fas.org

FAS is a group of scientists who work to promote the ethical and humanitarian use of technology by the U.S. government. It particularly focuses on national security issues, including intelligence. FAS maintains an extensive archive of governmental publications and other documents related to security issues on its Web site.

Foreign Policy Association (FPA)
470 Park Ave. S, 2nd Floor, New York, NY   10016
(212) 481-8100 • fax: (212) 481-9275

e-mail: info@fpa.org
Web site: www.fpa.org

FPA is a nonprofit organization that believes that a concerned and informed public is the foundation for an effective foreign policy. Publications such as the annual *Great Decisions* briefing book and the quarterly *Headline Series* review U.S. foreign policy issues, and FPA's *Global Q & A* series offers interviews with leading U.S. and foreign officials about terrorism, intelligence gathering, and a variety of other topics.

Heritage Foundation

214 Massachusetts Ave. NE, Washington, DC   20002-4999
(202) 546-4400 • fax: (202) 546-8328
e-mail: info@heritage.org
Web site: www.heritage.org

The foundation is a think tank that promotes conservative public policies, including a strong national defense. It sponsors research in numerous areas, including national security and intelligence reform, and maintains an extensive online archive of publications on national security issues. The foundation makes available a variety of publications, including backgrounders, lecture transcripts, op-eds, and special reports, on its Web site.

Hoover Institution

434 Galvez Mall, Stanford University
Stanford, CA   94305-6010
(650) 723-1754 • fax: (650) 723-1687
Web site: www.hoover.org

The Hoover Institution on War, Revolution, and Peace at Stanford University is a conservative public policy research center devoted to advanced study of politics, economics, and international affairs. The institution hosts world-renowned scholars and ongoing programs of policy-oriented research. Its many periodical publications include *Weekly Essays, Hoover Digest*, and *Policy Review* The Hoover Institution also publishes books, including *The Future of American Intelligence*, edited by Peter Berkowitz.

Institute for Policy Studies (IPS)
1112 16th Street NW, Suite 600, Washington, DC   20036
(202) 234-9382 • fax: (202) 387-7915
Web site: www.ips-dc.org

IPS is a progressive think tank that works to promote democracy and economic justice in the United States and around the world. In 1996 IPS partnered with the International Relations Center to form Foreign Policy in Focus, a think tank that is committed to advancing peace, justice, and international cooperation. Both Foreign Policy in Focus and IPS publish a variety of commentaries, briefings and reports.

International Relations Center (IRC)
PO Box 2178, Silver City, NM   88062-2178
(505) 388-0208
e-mail: irc@irc-online.org
Web site: www.irc-online.org

IRC is a progressive institute that was founded in 1979 in order to encourage a more socially responsible U.S. foreign policy. In 1996 IRC partnered with the International Relations Center to form Foreign Policy in Focus, a think tank that is committed to advancing peace, justice, and international cooperation. Both Foreign Policy in Focus and IRC publish a variety of commentaries, briefings and reports.

RAND Corporation
PO Box 2138, Santa Monica, CA   90407-2138
(310) 393-0411 • fax: (310) 393-4818
Web site: www.rand.org

RAND is a nonpartisan, nonprofit organization that seeks to improve policy and decision making through research and analysis. RAND was founded in 1948 in order to promote scientific research; it has since expanded into economic, political, and other types of research as well. RAND publishes commentaries, in-depth reports, and books on a variety of subjects, including foreign affairs, terrorism, and national security.

U.S. Department of State
2201 C St. NW, Washington, DC   20520
(202) 647-4000
Web site: www.state.gov

The State Department is a federal agency that advises the president on the formulation and execution of foreign policy. Congressional testimony and speeches given by State Department officials about intelligence-related issues, including the treatment of detainees and policies regarding renditions, are available on its Web site.

Bibliography

Books

Peter Berkowitz, ed.	*The Future of American Intelligence.* Stanford, CA: Hoover Institution Press, 2005.
Gary Berntsen and Ralph Pezzullo	*Jawbreaker: The Attack on Bin Laden and al-Qaeda: A Personal Account by the CIA's Key Field Commander.* New York: Crown, 2005.
William J. Daugherty	*Executive Secrets: Covert Action and the Presidency.* Lexington: University Press of Kentucky, 2004.
Tyler Drumheller and Elaine Monaghan	*On the Brink: An Insider's Account of How the White House Compromised American Intelligence.* New York: Carroll & Graf, 2006.
Stephen Grey	*Ghost Plane: The True Story of the CIA Torture Program.* New York: St. Martin's, 2006.
Seymour M. Hersh	*Chain of Command: The Road from 9/11 to Abu Ghraib.* New York: HarperCollins, 2004.
Loch K. Johnson and James J. Wirtz, editors	*Strategic Intelligence: Windows into a Secret World.* Los Angeles: Roxbury, 2004.
Ronald Kessler	*The CIA at War: Inside the Secret Campaign Against Terror.* New York: St. Martin's, 2003.

Alfred W. McCoy — *A Question of Torture: CIA Interrogation, from the Cold War to The War on Terror.* New York: Metropolitan, 2006.

Richard A. Posner — *Uncertain Shield: The U.S. Intelligence System in the Throes of Reform.* Lanham, MD: Rowman & Littlefield, 2006.

Gary C. Schroen — *First In: An Insider's Account of How the CIA Spearheaded the War on Terror in Afghanistan.* New York: Ballantine, 2005.

Jennifer E. Sims and Burton Gerber, eds. — *Transforming U.S. Intelligence.* Washington, DC: Georgetown University Press, 2005.

Periodicals:

Spencer Ackerman — "Under Analysis," *New Republic,* May 29, 2006.

David Bjerklie and Coco Masters — "How the CIA Can Be Fixed," *Time,* May 22, 2006.

Max Boot — "Derring-Do Becomes Don't," *Los Angeles Times,* July 22, 2004.

Mark Bowden — "The Dark Art of Interrogation," *Atlantic Monthly,* October 2003.

Saxby Chambliss — "We Have Not Correctly Framed the Debate on Intelligence Reform," *Parameters,* Spring 2005.

Alexander
Cockburn
"Politicize the CIA? You've Got to Be Kidding!" *Nation*, December 20, 2004.

Ivo Daalder and
Anthony Lake
"Smart Choices About Intelligence Reform," *Boston Globe*, August 19, 2004.

Charles N. Davis
"The Flaws in Intelligence Reform," *National Catholic Reporter*, December 24, 2004.

Michael Duffy
"How to Fix Our Intelligence," *Time*, April 26, 2004.

Economist
"How to Lose Friends and Alienate People," *Economist*, November 12, 2005.

Reuel Marc
Gerecht
"Against Rendition: Why the CIA Shouldn't Outsource Interrogations to Countries That Torture," *Weekly Standard*, May 16, 2005.

Michael A. Gips
"Spying Trouble," *Security Management*, August 2006.

Stephen Grey
"Torture's Tipping Point," *New Statesman*, December 19, 2005.

Stephen Grey
"Missing Presumed Tortured," *New Statesman*, November 20, 2006.

Efraim Halevy
"In Defence of the Intelligence Services: The Committees of Inquiry into American and British Intelligence Failures May Have Left the West Less Secure," *Economist*, July 31, 2004.

Stephen F. Hayes "The CIA 1, Bush 0: The Age of Reform Ends After 18 Months," *Weekly Standard*, May 22, 2006.

Nat Hentoff "What Kind of Country Are We?" *Progressive*, April 2005.

Michael Isikoff and Daniel Klaidman "Look Who's Not Talking—Still," *Newsweek*, April 4, 2005.

John B. Judis "CIA RIP," *New Republic Online*, December 20, 2005.

Jack Kelly "Ciao, CIA," *Pittsburgh Post-Gazette*, December 11, 2005.

Rich Lowry "Nothing Covert About It," *National Review Online*, May 19, 2006.

Khaled El-Masri "Extraordinary Rendition," *Harper's Magazine*, February 2006.

Herbert E. Meyer "What the CIA Doesn't See," *USA Today Magazine*, May 2004.

Dana Priest "Wrongful Imprisonment: Anatomy of a CIA Mistake," *Washington Post*, December 4, 2005.

Noam Scheiber "Speak Easy," *New Republic*, June 5, 2006.

Gary Schmitt "Less Central, More Intelligent? How Not to Reform the CIA," *Weekly Standard*, July 26, 2004.

Mark Steyn "The Death of Intelligence," *National Review*, December 27, 2004.

Gregory F. Treverton and Peter A. Wilson	"True Intelligence Reform Is Cultural, Not Just Organizational Chart Shift," *Christian Science Monitor*, January 13, 2005.
Jason Vest	"Destabilizing the CIA," *Nation*, December 13, 2004.

Index